new
Country style

new
Country style

Rubena Grigg

hamlyn

First published in Great Britain in 2001 by Hamlyn
a division of Octopus Publishing Group Ltd
2–4 Heron Quays, London E14 4JP

© Octopus Publishing Group Ltd 2001

Editor SHARON ASHMAN
Copy Editor JO LETHABY
Designer LOUISE GRIFFITHS
Senior Designer ROZELLE BENTHEIM
Production Controller LOUISE HALL

Photography DI LEWIS
Illustrator CARRIE HILL

ISBN 0 600 60155 2

A CIP record for this book is available from the
British Library

Printed and bound in China

10 9 8 7 6 5 4 3 2 1

Contents

Introduction

What is 'country style'? Simplicity, practicality and comfort are the intrinsic qualities of country style, which has a classic timelessness. It steers clear of sophisticated decoration with perfect finishes, and aims instead to reproduce an effect of age and faded elegance using a 'make-do-and-mend' philosophy. Simple curtains and slipcovers, practical floors, comfortable sofas and cushions – the style works well in homes in country settings, but looks equally effective in suburban homes, townhouses and city apartments. It is the look inside your home that matters, not where you live.

This book is deliciously inspiring and marks a new mood in country-style decorating. The *new* country-style look is fresh, crisp, simplistic and subtle. Out go overpowering colours, stripped pine and clutter. In come pale pretty florals, linens and sheers, distressed painted furniture and a simpler, uncrowded look. Opt for practical bare floors – painted, polished, limed or varnished with one of the latest environmentally friendly, water-based, low-odour and fast-drying products. Combine soft paint colours with fabrics based on vintage floral and paisley designs to unite an eclectic mix of furniture and accessories from yesteryear. No longer is it important to have a set of matching chairs, plates or cushions – it is far more stylish to have unusual oddments, which makes browsing around junk shops, markets, salvage and reclamation yards all the more fun. Old kitchen implements, glass, enamelware and mismatched china are all highly collectable and more easily found than real antiques.

Strong and hard-wearing, yet cool, soft and luxurious, linen is ideal for the new country-style look. Antique linen is very valuable and in great demand, especially if it is hand embroidered in the traditional way, white-on-white, or decorated with lace. Irish linen, along with that produced in France, is the finest in the world. International Antique Fairs (see Directory of Suppliers) are the best bet for antique linen sheets that won't break the bank. If you intend spending time in France or Belgium, try to plan your trip to coincide with one of the major European antiques (*brocante*) fairs. If that isn't possible, turn off the main routes and call into any country *brocante*, *dépôt-vente* or *grenier* that you see, often advertised by a noticeboard on the pavement. Some have

the appearance of a garage or a garden centre – don't be deterred, they can be full of treasures! There is room for bargaining, so have a price in your mind and stick to it. The hardest thing is to walk away if you have fallen in love with something! Only you can decide how much a piece is worth to you.

Wherever you find yourself, look out for floral china, white linen, original undecorated enamelware and pressed glass; scraps of old toiles – or choose from the wonderful array of new, faded-looking checks, stripes, spots, ginghams and floral fabrics; baskets and rush-seated chairs; rustic-painted furniture, ottomans, old cupboards and wardrobes; quilts, bedspreads, original eiderdowns, crisp linen sheets, old embroidered pillowcases and needlework. Look for anything that is vintage style with a touch of nostalgia.

This book is packed with projects that are grouped by room. Inspirational, informative and practical, it will appeal to anyone interested in creating the new country-style look in their home. The secret is to keep an eye out for treasures and recognize their potential, sometimes transforming an item into something quite spectacular, far removed from its original use.

Rubena Grigg

Hall

Rustic-looking paint finishes are a fast and effective way to cover walls and floors using the least amount of paint. The hall can suffer a lot of wear and tear, and tends to need redecorating more frequently than other rooms so why not create a slate-effect floor the next time around – all you need is emulsion paint. Continue the rustic theme with cushions made from natural hessian or an unusual linen scrim blind.

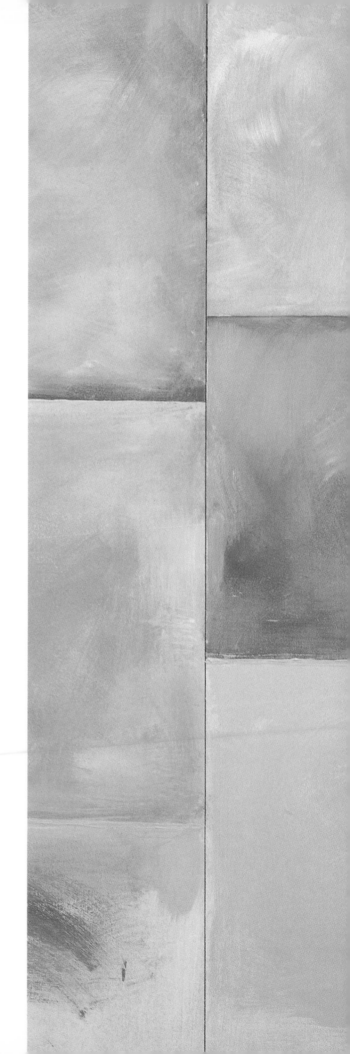

Rustic wall & floor

Very simple paint effects can be quickly and easily achieved with matt emulsion paint, to give bare walls and a floor of man-made material such as chipboard an authentic-looking rustic appearance.

   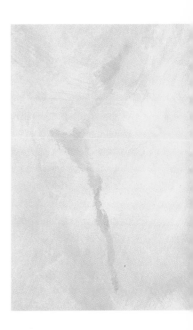

RUSTIC-LOOKING WALL
1 DAY

You will need

Matt emulsion paint in hessian/sack colour, plus a slightly darker brown (optional)
2.5cm (1in) household paintbrush
10cm (4in) household paintbrush
Old pâté or pie dish containing water
Kitchen paper

This rustic-looking paint finish is a fast and effective way to cover a wall using the least amount of paint. The wall illustrated here was painted in white matt emulsion paint first to provide a blank 'canvas'.

The simplest way to produce the desired paint finish is to have a dish of water beside the tin of paint as you work, rather than diluting all the paint at the outset. The dish needs to be substantial enough so that you can wipe the paint-loaded brush on the edge without the dish tipping over.

A little raw umber artist's acrylic tube paint can be added to matt emulsion paint to give an older, dustier look.

1. This first step is optional, but for a truly rustic look that simulates cracks and damp patches, begin by applying a little matt emulsion paint in a slightly darker colour than the hessian/sack colour you have chosen. Using the 2.5cm (1in) brush, paint realistic-looking 'damp patches' and 'cracks' in logical places – under windows, in the corners, where the ceiling meets the wall – or accentuate any unevenness already on the surface of the wall. Let these patches dry for a good half hour.

2. Dip the 10cm (4in) brush into the water first, removing the excess on the side of the dish if necessary, then into the hessian/sack coloured matt emulsion paint a little way. Brush the paint on to the wall, applying it with rough strokes in all directions. Over-brush these as necessary and continue until the entire wall is covered in rough brushstrokes. The brush should not be so wet that the paint runs down the wall. If this happens, brush out the runs and continue with less water, or dry off the brush before overbrushing the runs, being careful to use less water in future. A very small amount of

paint will spread over a wall, giving a lovely finish. (Use kitchen paper as necessary for cleaning up any dripped paint.)

3. Using the same quantities of paint and water as before, use the small paintbrush to paint a neat line along the top of the wall, where it meets the ceiling. Break up the straight lines by carefully criss-crossing a few strokes to blend in with the rest of the wall.

4. When you are satisfied with the first coat, stand back and look for any areas that may need a little alteration or improvement. If you think a second coat is necessary, let the first coat dry thoroughly first – this will take about 1 hour.

5. Once the walls are finished, you can paint the skirting boards, architraves, doors and windows similarly, providing they have a base coat of emulsion paint, or choose a flat oil-based paint from a heritage range to achieve a similar paint colour.

PAINTED 'SLATE' FLOOR – A Morning

You will need

Matt emulsion paint in white, plus small quantities of stone colours, for example burnt sienna or terracotta, mid/dark cream or fudge colour and pale cream
Large household paintbrush or roller with a long handle
7.5cm (3in) household paintbrush
Pencil
Straight length of wood or long rule
Dish of water
Kitchen paper
Narrow fitch or bristle brush – about 5mm (¼in)
Hard-wearing floor varnish (see text below)

Floors constructed from chipboard, medium-density fibreboard (MDF) or other man-made composite material can be very quickly and easily painted to give a more traditional look. The

floor illustrated here comprises 2450 x 600mm (8 x 2ft) lengths of chipboard laid side by side, each piece slotting into its neighbour like tongue-and-groove boards. The slight gaps between each piece, together with the rough edges, give the floor a realistic slab-like appearance when it is painted, and also dictate the width of each 'stone'. The surface of chipboard varies considerably – here, the coarser or rougher the surface the better.

The dull, flat finish of the matt emulsion paint really does give the appearance of a stone or slate floor – some of the flat swirling brushstrokes could be the marks of a slate-cutting machine. However, once varnished for really hard wear, this is bound to be lost to a certain degree.

There are many hard-wearing varnishes suitable for floors, particularly the acrylic varnishes, which require no upkeep once they are applied and allowed to dry and harden thoroughly, but they still have a semi-matt or

satin-like appearance. It would be possible to apply a hard-wearing acrylic gloss floor varnish – at least two coats – followed by two coats of flat matt varnish. Alternatively, you could leave the floor with its original emulsion paint finish and use a large rug and runners actually to walk on.

1. Paint the entire floor with the white matt emulsion paint, using a large brush or roller for the bulk of the floor and a smaller brush for painting up to the skirting boards. Apply at least two coats of paint, allowing the floor to dry thoroughly between coats.

2. Work out exactly how you intend to paint the floor: which areas to paint and where to begin, bearing in mind the amount of traffic that passes through your working space at peak times during the day, and taking into consideration the number of doors.

It is usually a good idea to begin against the skirting board along one wall, working along – and backwards. In some cases it

may be necessary to paint yourself out of a door. If the area is large or time is short, it may be advisable to work into the middle of the room, leaving the remainder to be completed the following day.

3. Using the pencil and straight edge, mark out squares or rectangles to denote the 'flagstones'. There is no need to measure them, but do ensure that by the final coat of paint the edges or dividing lines between each 'stone' are straight.

4. Have handy the materials you will be using – the three or four paint colours, a container of water to accommodate the larger brush and kitchen paper for cleaning up. It is best to use the darkest shade as a base, working up layer by layer to the lightest colours. For each layer of colour, use as little paint as possible. Dip only the tip of the large brush into the colour and drag it across the surface to spread the paint in a thin layer. If it becomes too wet or heavy, wash and dry off the brush on kitchen paper, and use only the smallest amount of water on the brush to spread it roughly again. This technique usually shows up the chips of wood on the surface of the board and gives an authentically rustic rough stone appearance.

5. Begin by roughly painting your chosen base colour on the first few 'stones' – the colour variation created by rough, uneven, brushstrokes adds interest and helps create a realistic 'rustic' effect. Some of the original white-painted floor

will show through, which helps create the impression of layers and resembles slate, which itself comprises many layers.

Pull the brush sideways along its narrowest edge to form the 'edge' of each 'stone', going over the pencil lines. These painted lines will look fairly rough at this stage. Leave the paint to dry.

6. Apply a lighter shade of paint in another thin layer as before, keeping within the edges of each 'stone'. Repeat with another one or two layers of lighter coloured paint in the same way, allowing the paint to dry thoroughly between applications.

7. If you have enough space in which to work, you can begin painting the base colours of the next section of 'stones' before completing the first section. Once under way, you will devise a type of conveyor belt system to speed up the process, but do not get carried away to the point where you cannot reach the sections that need to be finished unless you kneel or tread on wet paint!

Stand back occasionally and look at the overall effect of the 'stones' and make any necessary adjustments. The overall effect is more important than getting just one particular 'stone' perfect.

8. Once a good number of 'stones' are dry, take up the narrow fitch or bristle brush. Dip

the brush in the paint (a contrasting colour can work well) and, with the help of your straight edge or rule, paint a line to accentuate the division between the 'stones'. Leave to dry.

9. Complete the floor with at least two coats of your chosen floor varnish.

PAINTED CUPBOARD

The pine cupboard shown here originally had a plain paint finish. A transformation was achieved by sanding the cupboard with 100 grade sandpaper to form a key on which to paint. Three or four coats of thinned acrylic primer undercoat were applied until the finish looked good. After each undercoat had dried, the edges of the cupboard top and doors were sanded through to simulate areas of wear. Finally, three slightly thinned coats of almond white matt emulsion paint were applied and left to dry.

The cupboard was then made to look older by rubbing on a dark wax furniture polish, which spreads better if you apply a natural white or clear beeswax polish at the same time. By applying both waxes to the cloth it is easier to avoid unsightly patches of dark that refuse to spread.

This polished surface is hard-wearing. A snippet of antique fabric can be tied around the door handle to brighten it up.

Linen scrim blind

This simple blind is made from natural linen scrim. Linen braid is sewn across the top, through which is threaded a long length of plaited hand-spun Jacob wool combined with the long linen threads pulled from the bottom edge of the blind, which form the attractive frayed edge.

2 HOURS

You will need

Length of natural linen scrim, about 160cm (63in) wide or according to your window's dimensions (see text below)
Tape measure
Sharp scissors
Length of linen braid or trim with holes to thread through
Long glass-headed pins
Sewing machine or needle
Matching thread
Skein or ball of hand-spun Jacob wool, or wool with a similar appearance
Large safety pin or hairgrip
3 cut nails

To continue the rustic theme the blind is held up by three ancient cut nails. These have been driven into the wooden frame, one either side of the window for securing the 'drawstring' plait with knots and one in the middle to support the blind and prevent it from sagging.

To determine the quantity of linen scrim required, measure the height of the window from where the top of the blind will begin when it is attached to the nails. Cut the fabric about 7.5cm (3in) longer than this measurement. (The sides of the linen scrim come already machine stitched to avoid further fraying.)

1. Carefully pull out any loose threads along the edge of the scrim that will be the top of the blind, leaving a frayed edge of about 12mm (½in) and retaining any long threads to incorporate into the woollen plait.

2. Pull the long threads carefully one or two at a time from what will be the bottom edge of the blind, leaving a frayed edge of approximately 4cm (1½in) and again saving the threads.

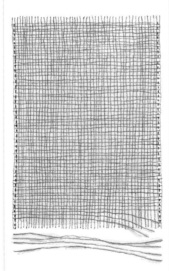

3. Cut a length of linen braid or trim to match the width of the blind, allowing extra for turnings at either end so that the holes line up when the ends are turned under.

4. Pin the braid along the top edge of the blind, 2.5cm (1in) away from the edge. Machine or hand stitch in place along both long edges of the braid, parallel with the top edge of the blind.

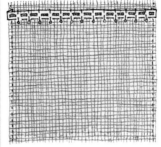

5. To make the decorative woollen plait for the top of the blind, measure the width of the blind and add to this measurement an extra 20-23cm (8-9in) at either end for knotting the plait and tying it around the nails. Cut the hand-spun wool into long lengths to match the measurement – you may need to use three for each strand of the plait so that the finished plait does not look too thin.

6. Knot together three thick strands of wool and the reserved linen threads – if you have sufficient these can be divided between the three strands; if not, add them along with one strand of the plait only. Secure the knotted end with long glass-headed pins pushed into the back of an easy chair or other suitable object. Plait the strands evenly and secure with a knot when you reach the end.

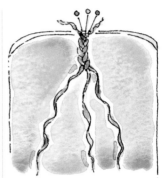

7. Take the finished plait and attach a safety pin or hairgrip to one end. Thread this through the linen braid on the blind, drawing in the blind slightly if necessary to suit the size of your window.

8. To hang the blind, tap three attractive old cut nails into the window frame. Wind the plaited woollen thread around the two outside nails a few times and tie in loose knots to secure. Support the middle of the blind on the centre nail.

Hessian cushions

These simple country-style cushions are made from natural jute hessian. The inside of the laced cushion is cut from an old ecru-coloured French linen sheet that had become worn in the middle. Anything in natural soft white fabric would be suitable, such as raw cotton, linen, duck, drill or peasant cotton.

CUSHION WITH PLAITED TRIM – A MORNING

You will need

Tape measure
Sharp scissors
Piece of jute hessian
Square cushion pad
Long glass-headed pins
Large-eyed tapestry needle or
    larding needle
Skein or ball of hand-spun Jacob
    wool, or wool with a similar
    appearance
Safety pin
2 antique pearl buttons

1. Cut out two squares of hessian, 5cm (2in) larger all round than the cushion pad.

2. Pull out some threads to fray all four edges by 12mm (½in).

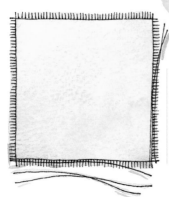

3. Lay one hessian square on the work surface in front of you and centre the cushion pad on top.

4. Lay the second hessian square on top and pin the two squares together all round the cushion pad, taking care not to catch the pad in the pins.

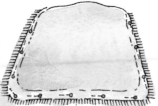

5. Thread the needle with a single strand of the Jacob wool and make a substantial knot at the end to stop it pulling through the open weave of the hessian. Sew the cushion cover together with long, even, fairly loose running stitches, keeping the stitches as straight as possible and removing the pins as you work. Fasten off the wool securely when finished.

6. For the decorative plait made from the hand-spun Jacob wool, measure the length of one side of the cushion pad. Multiply this by five and add another 7.5cm (3in); this allows for a long enough plait to go around all four sides of the cushion cover, plus sufficient for the fourth side to be intertwined twice with both ends knotted and trimmed off.

7. Cut three strands of Jacob wool to match this measurement, one length for each strand of the plait; knot the three strands together at one end. Secure the knotted end with two or three long glass-headed pins pushed into the back of an easy chair or other suitable object (see Step 6, Linen Scrim Blind, page 15). Plait the strands together evenly and secure with a knot when you reach the end.

8. Take the finished plait and attach a safety pin to one end. Thread the plait through the running stitches around the outside of one side of the cushion cover.

9. When you have threaded it around all four sides, intertwine the plait back along the last side through to its end. Readjust the knot if necessary and trim both knots to look tidy and the same length. Attach an antique pearl button to one corner of the cover.

10. To complete the cushion, make a second plait and decorate the other side of the cushion in the same way.

LACED HESSIAN
CUSHION – A MORNING

You will need

Tape measure
Sharp scissors
Piece of antique linen or white
    cotton remnant
Long glass-headed pins
Sewing machine (optional)
Needle and white thread
35.5cm (14in) square
    cushion pad
0.5m (½yd) jute hessian
Skein or ball of hand-spun
    Jacob wool, or wool with a
    similar appearance
Large-eyed tapestry needle
    or larding needle

1. Cut out two 38cm (15in) squares of antique linen or white cotton. With right sides facing, pin the pieces of fabric together around three sides, allowing 12mm (½in) for the seams, then machine or hand stitch.

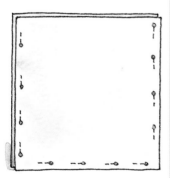

2. Turn the fabric the right side out and turn in and press the 12mm (½in) seam allowance along the cover opening. Insert the cushion pad. Pin then sew the opening closed with small neat hand stitches.

3. Cut out two 38cm (15in) squares of hessian. Carefully remove a few threads around all four edges of each hessian square, leaving frayed edges up to 2cm (¾in) deep.

4. Sandwich the white linen- or cotton-covered cushion between the two squares of hessian. Cut a long length of wool and tie one end in a substantial knot, large enough not to pull through the open weave of the hessian. Thread the other end through a large-eyed needle and, using a neat over-and-over stitch, work around all four edges of the cushion, lacing the two squares of hessian together. Allow the cushion to protrude a little for effect. Secure the end of the wool well to finish.

Glazed cupboard

Old pieces, such as this glazed, stained oak display cupboard, are ideal for a complete makeover with emulsion paint and wax. The finishing touch is the hand-crocheted antique linen lace glued to the shelf fronts, its open-work design allowing the rose madder paint used on the cupboard shelves to show through.

A WEEKEND

You will need

Old glazed cupboard in need of renovation
100 grade sandpaper
Chemical varnish stripper (optional)
Shellac varnish and old paintbrush
2.5cm (1in) household paintbrushes
White acrylic primer undercoat
5mm (¼in) fitch or No. 8 artist's paintbrush
Matt emulsion paint in rose madder, or a colour of your choice, and almond white
Natural beeswax polish with a little dark wax furniture polish added
Soft cloth
Hot glue gun and glue stick
Sharp scissors
Antique linen lace
Tape measure

The cupboard illustrated here had a 1940s or 50s look about it when it was purchased very reasonably at an auction. After sanding, the cupboard was painted inside and out with several coats of white acrylic primer undercoat. However, the oak stain bled into the paint so two coats of shellac varnish were then applied to create a barrier before continuing. It is therefore advisable to use shellac varnish from the start as outlined in the steps below.

The cupboard that was used here has a decorative recess around the glazing, which was carefully painted towards the very end of the project with a narrow paintbrush.

1. Remove the shelves from the cupboard and sand the cupboard and the shelves by hand using 100 grade sandpaper to remove the varnish. Alternatively, if the varnish on your cupboard is very shiny and thick, use a chemical varnish stripper, wearing the appropriate protective clothing and following the manufacturer's instructions carefully.

2. Remove all the dust from inside the cupboard and along the door frames, using a vacuum cleaner. Wipe clean.

3. If your cupboard has a dark woodstain, you will need to apply shellac varnish to create a barrier and prevent the stain bleeding into the paint that you will be applying. Allow the first coat to dry (usually about half an hour in a warm environment) before applying a second coat of shellac. Leave to dry.

4. Using a 2.5cm (1in) household paintbrush, paint the cupboard inside and out with acrylic primer undercoat. Also paint the shelves on both sides and on the edges – these can be painted on one side and edge at a time and stood up to dry thoroughly before

completing the coat. Use a fitch or artist's paintbrush to paint the mouldings around the glazing. Allow the paint to dry thoroughly before applying a second and possibly a third coat, until the cupboard and shelves have a good, dense covering of white. Leave to dry thoroughly.

5. Paint the inside of the cupboard, including the backs of the glazed doors, and the shelves (again on both sides and edges) using rose madder matt emulsion paint or a colour of your choice, applying at least two coats. Allow the paint to dry thoroughly after each coat.

6. Apply two or three coats of almond white matt emulsion paint to the outside surfaces of the cupboard. As always, leave the paint to dry thoroughly after each coat before applying the next.

7. When the final coat of paint is completely dry, gently rub a mixture of natural beeswax polish and a dark wax furniture polish over the paintwork, using a soft cloth, to tone down the 'newness' of the paint. (Applying both waxes to the cloth makes it easier to avoid unsightly patches of dark polish that refuse to spread out evenly.)

8. Heat the hot glue gun. Cut a length of lace for each cupboard shelf, allowing 12mm (1/2in) extra for turning under the lace at each end of the shelves. Apply the hot glue directly to the shelf edge to avoid burning your fingers, and stick the lace edging in place carefully.

WHITE WOODSTAINED FLOOR – A DAY

If you hanker for a stylishly up-to-the-minute bare wooden floor that is light, clean and hard-wearing, try this wonderful Finnish product, a sealant and a hard varnish, to which you can add lovely soft colours from the same range (see Directory of Suppliers, page 122). Once applied, the finish requires no maintenance other than washing and keeping clean. Whether your floors are newly laid softwood or lovely old boards that have been sanded, this product provides a finish that is ideal for both. The other big advantage is that it is water-based and therefore dries quickly, so the floor need not be out of use for long while you complete the job.

1. Apply three coats of birch-white woodstain to the floorboards, followed by two coats of the supreme varnish, making sure each application is allowed to dry thoroughly before continuing with the next coat. The end result is a floor with a lovely translucent white appearance, which shows up the knots and the grain of the wood beautifully.

2. If your floorboards are discoloured in any way, you could mix the woodstain with a little white emulsion paint to ensure that the boards are well covered. Empty the thick milky-looking water-based woodstain into an open container, and have an open can of white matt emulsion paint positioned beside it. Dip the brush into the woodstain first and spread it on the boards, then into the emulsion to paint on to the floorboards, then dip the brush back into the stain and so on. When you have finished working on the floorboards the wood grain will still show through, but the density of white will be greater.

Kitchen

Simple-to-make stylish curtains; up-to-the-minute ticking checks and stripes for chair seats; antique striped linen tea towels and vintage fabrics for colourful cushions – these pages are packed with wonderful ideas to transform your kitchen.

Tea towel slipcover

This is an attractive way to cover a shabby chair or to protect a newly upholstered chair from pets. These lovely old, robust, heavy-duty linen tea towels edged in a double red stripe come in generous sizes and are already hemmed so there is little work required to make the slipcovers. You could easily make a second set and have summery-looking slipcovers for a seasonal change of scene.

A MORNING

You will need

2 antique striped linen tea towels
Chair to be covered
Long glass-headed pins
Sharp scissors
Tape measure
Sewing machine / needle and
*   matching thread*
Small remnant of red-and-cream
*   ticking*

The remnant of red-and-cream ticking is used to make the ties for the slipcover – four for the seat piece and four for the chair back. An alternative is to use eight lengths of cotton webbing, the ends of which will need turning under to prevent fraying.

1. Open out a tea towel and centre it over the chair seat, right side uppermost, ensuring that an equal amount of fabric hangs down at each side and at the front of the chair. Push a couple of long glass-headed pins through the tea towel and into the chair seat to hold it in position temporarily.

2. At the front corners, tuck the excess side fabric beneath the front 'flap' to form a pleat. Secure the two layers of fabric together temporarily with pins.

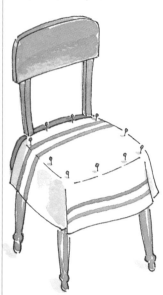

3. Take the second tea towel and cut 27cm (10½in) off one end of it – this smaller piece is for the back flap piece that holds the seat cover in place. Measure the width of the chair seat between the upright struts of the chair back to determine the width of the back flap piece. The finished flap has a stripe each side of it, so decide how much of the plain

central section needs to be removed before the two striped sections can be rejoined to make the desired width. Mark cutting guidelines with a few pins.

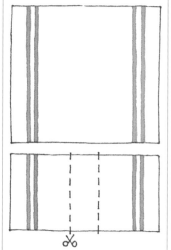

4. Cut the piece of tea towel as marked and machine zigzag stitch the raw edge on each striped piece to prevent fraying. Place these two zigzagged edges together, right sides facing. Pin then machine stitch.

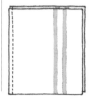

5. Open out and press the central seam open. Turn the remaining raw edge over twice to make a neat hem. Hand or machine stitch and press.

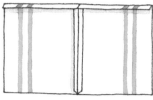

6. Slide the back flap beneath the tea towel already on the chair seat and adjust it until it is aligned correctly with the overhanging fabric at the sides of the chair. Attach the flap to the main piece with a couple of pins.

7. Remove the slipcover from the chair and spread it out on your work surface. Pin the back flap to the main piece properly, then secure it by machine stitching along the edge of the main tea towel. Replace the slipcover on the chair and recheck the two front corner pleats. Adjust until they sit well, then remove the cover once more and secure the corners with a few neat hand stitches.

8. Use the remaining two-thirds of the second tea towel for the chair back cover. Fold it in half and hang it over the back of the chair to determine the required width. Reduce the width if necessary, as you did for the seat back flap, by removing the excess fabric from the middle and rejoining the striped pieces (see Steps 4 and 5 above). Turn the raw edge over twice to make a neat hem and hand or machine stitch as before.

9. Fold the tea towel in half, right sides facing, pin then machine stitch the sides of the cover. Turn the cover the right side out and press.

10. For the slipcover ties, cut eight long strips measuring 30 x 5cm (12 x 2in) from the ticking remnant. Turn under 12mm (½in) all round each strip to neaten the raw edges and press. Then fold each strip in half lengthways, right side facing outwards, and press. Pin then machine topstitch close to the edge (see Steps 13 and 14, Linen Curtains with Striped Edge, page 35).

11. Replace both the slipcovers on the chair to determine the positions for the ties. Pin in place, then remove the covers and machine topstitch the ties neatly to the covers.

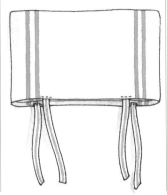

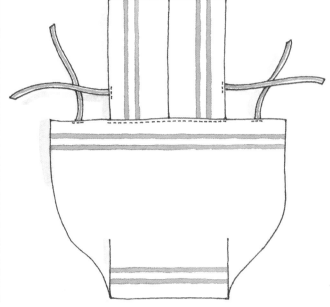

Striped floral cushions

Antique striped French linen tea towels combined with printed fabric in eye-catching colours make stunning cushion covers. This pretty rose print was removed from three old door panels. After careful handwashing and ironing, the fragile floral fabric was hand sewn on to the tea towel. A remnant of equally pretty new fabric could easily be used instead.

AN EVENING

You will need

Antique striped linen tea towel
Tape measure
Sharp scissors
Remnant of floral fabric
Long glass-headed pins
Sewing machine / needle and matching thread
Buttons or touch-and-close tape (optional)
Small flattish pillow or cushion pad

Antique linen tea towels are usually large, often measuring 60 x 90cm (24 x 36in), and can make very generous-sized cushion covers. Use a small flat pillow or a longish cushion inside the cushion cover, or alternatively you can make your own cushion pad to fit.

1. Press the tea towel. Use a tape measure to determine the areas of the tea towel to which the floral fabric will be attached. Cut a panel of the floral fabric to size, allowing an extra 12mm (½in) all round for turning under the edges. Turn these edges under and press.

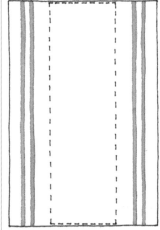

2. Pin the floral fabric on to the right side of the tea towel. Machine topstitch the fabric in place, or sew it by hand if the fabric is fragile. Press.

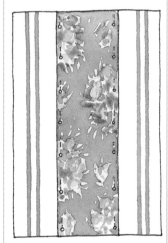

3. Place the tea towel in front of you, right side uppermost and fold over one end towards the middle. Bring the other end over the first end to overlap it by about 20cm (8in). Pin these short sides of the cushion cover then machine stitch.

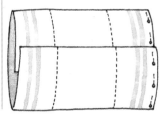

4. Turn the tea towel the right side out. Since both ends of the tea towel are hemmed, the cushion cover can be left as it is as long as it is not overstuffed. Alternatively, add a fastening for the opening. Make one or two buttonholes in the overlapping flap and sew buttons on the corresponding part of the opening, or hand stitch a strip of touch-and-close tape along the edges of the opening.

5. Insert a suitable small flattish pillow or cushion pad to finish the cushion.

Linen curtains with striped edge

Simple cream-painted walls are a perfect backdrop for these lovely home-made linen curtains with smart red striped edges. They are made up from antique linen sheets and a manglecloth (see page 24), cut in half lengthways so as to retain the edge stripe for use on each curtain.

A DAY

You will need

Tape measure
Sharp scissors
2 ecru-coloured antique French linen single sheets or a double sheet cut in half
Long glass-headed pins
Sewing machine and needle
Matching thread
Antique European linen manglecloth

The linen fabric for the curtains needs to be medium- to heavyweight but soft. An alternative to linen sheets is to use a pair of inexpensive shop-bought linen/cotton mix curtains. The manglecloth used here was 90cm (36in) wide, which is narrow in relation to its length of 2.5m (2¾yd). The majority of windows would require this to be shortened for use as curtains.

1. The first step is to measure the height of the window and determine accurately the finished length of your curtains, remembering to allow for the curtain loops as you make your calculations. Add to this measurement an extra 10–15cm (4–6in) for the hem.

2. Measure the width of the window and use this measurement to decide whether your curtains require one and a half or two widths (drops) of fabric. Cut the required number of fabric widths to the length that you determined in Step 1. To join the fabric widths, place them together, right sides facing, pin along the seam line then machine stitch. Press the seam flat.

3. Lay the manglecloth on a large work surface and smooth it out flat. Lay the prepared linen sheets against the manglecloth to determine the correct length for the latter. The manglecloth side border strips need to be very slightly longer than the linen curtain lengths, as the top and bottom edges of the border strips will be folded over the edges of the linen.

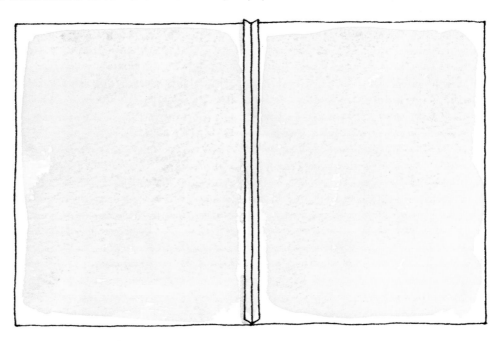

4. Mark all cutting lines on the manglecloth with pins as follows. If the manglecloth needs shortening, decide how much excess fabric is to be removed from the length and mark most of it to come from the striped end section at the top end of the cloth. Remove the striped end at the bottom of the manglecloth only if the curtains are short ones. These excess pieces will be used for making the striped curtain loops – you need to retain as much as possible of the striped end cloth for the loops.

To produce the pieces required for the curtains' striped side edges, measure and mark a cutting line on the manglecloth, 20cm (8in) in from each side edge and parallel with it. This leaves a central section of plain fabric – 50cm (20in) wide in this case – which will be used to make the plain curtain loops and the top borders.

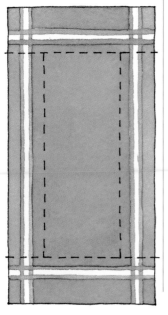

5. Cut out the two long side border strips. Their 20cm (8in) width allows for 2cm (³⁄₄in) turnings each side, which leaves a finished striped border trim of 16.5cm (6¹⁄₂in). Since the stripe runs close to the edge of the manglecloth, when the raw side edge is turned in the stripe will be on the edge, close against the linen panel.

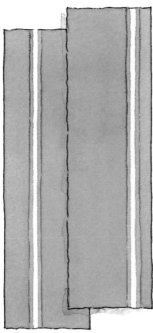

6. Lay the pressed linen curtains on your work surface, right side uppermost. Decide and mark which is to be the left-hand curtain and which the right, as it is all too easy to end up with two curtains the same! Down the edge of both curtains where they will meet in the centre of the window, measure and mark with pins a guideline, 16.5cm (6¹⁄₂in) in from the side edge and parallel with it.

7. With right sides facing, pin the striped edge of a side border strip to the front face of each curtain, aligning the seam along the pinned guideline, as illustrated. Machine stitch.

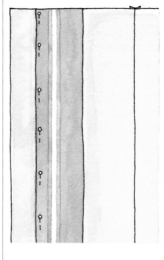

8. Turn each side border strip to the right side over the front of the linen curtain so that its right side is facing outwards. Press flat. Fold the remaining overlapping fabric along the side, top and bottom edges of the border strip to the back, over the edges of the curtain, and press. Pin in place before neatly slipstitching on the back of the curtain.

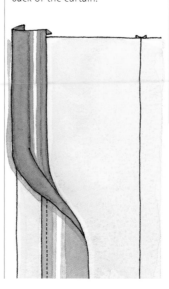

9. To make the border for the top of the curtains, cut several 15cm (6in) widths from the plain, unstriped remnants, pinning and machining them together to make two long strips, each long enough to edge the top of a curtain. Press all the joining seams flat then turn under 12mm (¹⁄₂in) all round each strip to neaten the raw edges and press. Fold each border strip in half lengthways, right side facing outwards, and press.

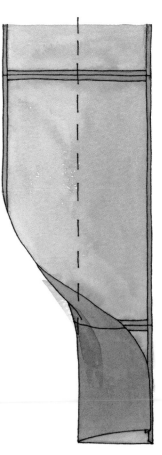

10. Slip a long folded top border strip over the top edge of each curtain, placing one end snugly against the striped side border strip of the curtain.

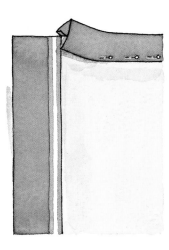

11. Pin in place then machine topstitch close to the edges of the border strip.

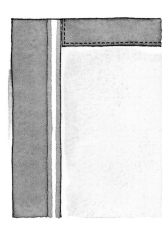

12. To make the curtain loops, measure the width of your curtains and allow for a loop every 25cm (10in). (The curtains illustrated are 150cm/60in wide and each has ten loops; the two on the striped side border are closer together so as to match up the stripes.) Cut a sufficient number of strips of fabric, 12.5 x 25cm (5 x 10in), utilizing every bit of striped fabric possible and

making at least two vertically striped loops – one to match up with the striped side border on each curtain.

13. Turn under 12mm (½in) or less around each strip to neaten the raw edges, and press. Fold each strip in half lengthways, right side facing outwards, press.

14. Pin then machine topstitch in place.

15. When all the strips are completed, fold them in half to form loops. Position a striped loop to line up with each striped side border strip. Distribute the remaining striped loops as evenly as possible among the plain ones to brighten up the curtains with touches of colour.

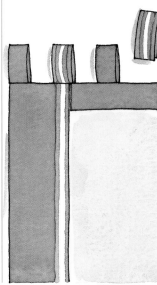

16. Pin the loops to the wrong side of the curtain. Allow about 10cm (4in) of each loop to protrude above the curtain top. Machine stitch two rows of stitches parallel with the curtain top edge to secure the loops firmly, stitching one row along the top edge of the curtain and the second close to the ends of the loops.

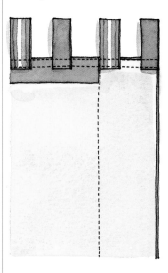

17. Lay the curtains on your work surface to measure the exact finished length – marking with pins at intervals. Turn up the hem, folding in the corners neatly; pin and slipstitch by hand, taking care the stitches are not visible from the front of the curtains. Press the curtains well before threading the loops on to the curtain pole.

Sitting room

These ideas are stunningly attractive, yet simple and inexpensive ways to transform large areas. Alter the look of your sitting room without changing the furniture – antique linen sheets, a colourful quilt and fresh fabrics help to achieve an entirely new country-style makeover.

Marble effect floor

If you are impatient for quick results and instant colour on your floor, this fast-drying paint finish, which reproduces the effect of marble slabs in soft greys, blues and slatey greens, is the perfect answer – if a little hard on the knees to apply!

3 DAYS

You will need

Matt emulsion paint in white and soft blue/grey, plus small quantities of colours such as ultramarine blue, dark blue/grey, soft pale turquoise, green and light grey
Roller with a long handle
5cm (2in) household paintbrush
Old cushion or piece of foam
Pencil
Straight length of wood or long rule
7.5cm (3in) household paintbrush
Plastic cartons with lids
PVA adhesive
Old tablespoon
Large natural sea sponge
Kitchen paper
Lightweight gloves
Clear, non-yellowing water-based specialist floor varnish

The floor illustrated here is 50m² (60sq yd), constructed from 2450 x 600mm (8 x 2ft) lengths of chipboard, and is a less expensive alternative to solid wooden flooring. This floor took three days to paint, which included applying two coats of hard-wearing floor varnish.

Since the lengths of chipboard are laid like tongue-and-groove panelling, there are slight gaps between them. The pieces of chipboard dictate the width of each 'marble slab' and, when divided into squares and rectangular shapes, their rough edges give the floor a realistic slab-like appearance. It does not matter that the surface of the chipboard over different pieces may vary from coarse to smooth.

When you are working with the sponge and dipping it into the glaze and assorted paint colours, it is a good idea to wash the sponge out every so often as otherwise the paint will begin to look like mud. Whenever you stop working with the sponge, wash it in warm soapy water then rinse it thoroughly in clear water, otherwise the PVA adhesive will turn it rock hard. Scrubbed-out margarine cartons with lids make ideal plastic containers for paint and glaze. The lids can be replaced if you take a break, preventing the paint or glaze from drying out.

1. Paint the entire chipboard floor with white matt emulsion paint (or any other white water-based paint), using a roller for the bulk of the floor and a 5cm (2in) paintbrush for painting up to the skirting boards. Leave the paint to dry before applying a second coat. Two coats of paint are necessary to provide a good base on which to work.

2. Have handy all the materials you will be using to paint the floor. You will need to work across the floor by moving backwards away from a wall – it may be best to start at the far end of the room away from the main entrance door(s). Find a comfortable old cushion or a piece of foam on which to kneel. Starting from the skirting board and working backwards, use the pencil and straight edge to draw lines across the chipboard lengths and mark out two or three rows of 'marble slabs'. The 'slabs' can be in all different

sizes – no 'slab' is exact but the lines between them do need to be straight.

3. Use a 7.5cm (3in) household paintbrush on its narrowest edge to paint around the edges of each 'slab', then roughly paint on your chosen base colours. To give the slabs sharper edges, pull the brush loaded with the relevant colour along the wooden straight edge, cleaning the paint off it each time before proceeding. The colour variation adds interest and looks realistic. A long line or sizeable section of 'slabs' can be painted at one time, but do remember to allow yourself plenty of room to return to the first section when you want to begin sponging on the glaze for the marble effect, otherwise you will inevitably find yourself kneeling on wet paint.

4. Next, make up the emulsion glaze in a plastic carton, mixing equal parts of soft blue/grey emulsion paint and PVA adhesive with up to four parts water. Spoon two tablespoons of each of the other colours you are using into separate cartons.

5. Rinse the sponge in clean water to soften it, then squeeze it in kitchen paper to remove the excess water. Wearing lightweight gloves, dip the tip of the sponge into the prepared emulsion glaze before dipping it into a colour. Sponge all over the first 'slab', working as near to its edges as possible – if you go over on to a neighbouring slab of a different colour, wipe off the unwanted paint with kitchen paper. Now dip the sponge into

another colour and sponge over the slab again to get a lovely effect where the two colours merge. If the base colour is dark, dip the sponge into the glaze first then the same dark colour and sponge over the slab. You could then dip the sponge into the white and build up a layered effect – you will soon discover the combination of colours that works best.

6. Sponge several 'slabs' in this way, always dipping the sponge into the glaze first each time before dipping it into the required colour, otherwise the effect will be lost. Do not expect the marbled effect to appear immediately as you work; you may have to sponge over the 'slabs' several times, allowing the

paint to dry a little in between sponging. You will need to keep replenishing the cartons of paint and glaze as you work. Stand back to check your work now and then so that you can make any adjustments necessary. However, the overall effect of the 'marbled' floor is more important than individual 'slabs'.

7. While waiting for the first section of 'marble slabs' to dry, you could use the time to mark out the next section using the pencil and straight edge.

8. When you have finished painting and sponging all the 'slabs', leave the floor to dry out thoroughly overnight.

9. The next day, take a 7.5cm

(3in) paintbrush and prepare to begin work at the same starting point and work away from the wall as before. Apply a generous coat of absolutely clear (although it may look milky), non-yellowing hard varnish, according to the manufacturer's directions. Leave to dry for the recommended length of time before applying a second coat of varnish.

10. Do be patient in allowing the floor to dry thoroughly before replacing the furniture. An emulsion glaze is a very hard-wearing paint finish, particularly when varnished with a specialist floor varnish, but any heavy furniture dragged into position just a few hours after the varnish has been applied will damage the newly painted floor.

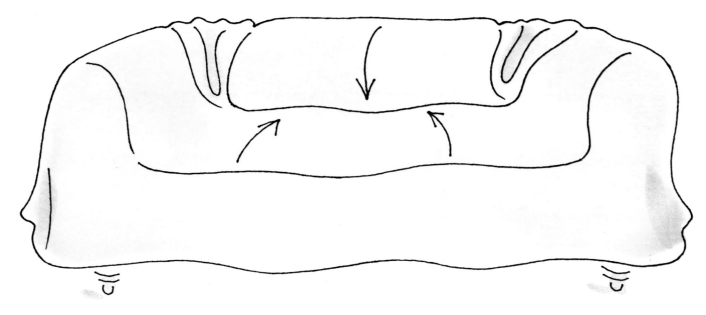

4. Make deep pleats or folds in the sheet to fit it neatly inside the back corners of the sofa.

5. To keep the ends of the sofa looking tidy, pull up the excess sheet at each end of the sofa and fold it deeply underneath itself so that the sheet is doubled back on itself over the sofa arms. This will take up the excess fabric and give you two 'ends' that can be knotted together. Tuck in the folded sheet deeply between the base of the arms and the seat.

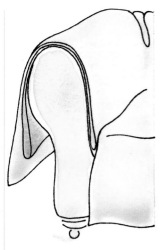

LINEN

Linen is so long-lasting that linen tablecloths and napkins, bedlinen and curtains have become family heirlooms. From coarse canvas to the finest lawn or gauze, all antique linen is expensive due to its rarity value. Retail outlets tend to charge extortionate prices so antique fairs are well worth visiting for better bargains. When choosing antique linen sheets, always carefully unfold the beautifully laundered, seemingly perfect sheets to check for weak spots, holes and immovable stains.

6. Now experiment with the two 'ends' of fabric that are to be knotted together to find the best look for your sofa. It may be that you can bring both 'ends' upwards and out at an angle, bringing some of the underneath fabric out, over the front of the sofa arms, to form attractive creases or folds that drape around each arm.

7. Once you are satisfied with the positioning and look of the knots, replace the seat cushions neatly on the sofa if you have removed them.

8. Open out the second, better sheet, ready to use lengthways this time, so that its central seam runs from the back to the front of the sofa. Fold under the side edges of this sheet as necessary so that it fits the width of the sofa seat and back, inside the sofa arms.

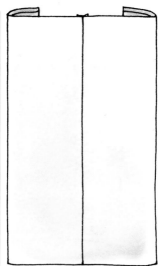

9. Stand behind the sofa and align one end of the sheet with the bottom edge of the sofa back as before. Bring the sheet over the sofa back and tuck it in deeply at the base of the inside back, this time over the top of the seat cushions, then continue it down to the front edge of the sofa. Stand back to check that the top sheet is level and square.

Ticking

Navy and white are a cl[...]
cushions on a French day[...]
navy-and-white ticking. [...]
used for featherbeds or n[...]
new designs available.

LAVENDER TICKING CUSHION – 1 HOUR

You will need

Sharp scissors
Tape measure
Piece of ticking
*Piece of muslin or gauze plus loose
        dried lavender, or small
        quantity of wadding or other
        suitable cushion filling*
Long glass-headed pins
*Sewing machine / needle and
        matching thread*
Several fresh stems of lavender

The w[...]
deep [...]
freshl[...]
on a s[...]
the ro[...]
detail [...]
group [...]
To fill [...]
lavend[...]
gauze [...]
to mak[...]
contain[...]

1. Cut [...]
rectang[...]
25 x 46[...]
then cu[...]
in the m[...]

2. Cut a[...]
the pock[...]
3½in), w[...]
in the op[...]
those on [...]
Turn all f[...]
neaten th[...]
then sew [...]
hand stitc[...]

3. Pin the [...]
position on [...]
rectangle [...]
on one hal[...]
large piece[...]

PIPED TICKING CUSHION – AN EVENING

You will need

Sharp scissors
Tape measure
*0.5m (½yd) striped ticking,
        120–137cm (48–54in) wide*
Pencil
*Straight length of wood or long
        rule*
Long glass-headed pins
*Sewing machine with standard
        and piping foot*
Needle and white thread
*Approx. 1.5m (1¾yd) piping
        cord*
33cm (13in) square cushion pad

Piping, or corded edging, gives a
smart finish to the cushion. It
requires strips of the striped
ticking to be cut diagonally (on
the bias) and joined together so
as to cover the piping cord. This
forms an interesting edge as the
stripes then run in a different
direction to those on the main
part of the cushion cover.

1. Measure and cut out two 35.5cm (14in) squares of striped ticking.

2. Lay the remaining ticking in front of you, wrong side uppermost. Using a pencil and straight edge, lightly mark lines diagonally across the fabric, at an angle of 45° to the selvage and 5cm (2in) apart. These denote the cutting lines for the binding strips of fabric that will be used to cover the piping cord. The length of the strips will be dictated by the width of the fabric available – you need enough strips to make one long strip of binding equal to the circumference of the cushion, allowing for a seam allowance of 12mm (½in) for every join.

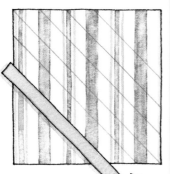

3. Cut out the strips of fabric and stitch them together to make one long strip of binding. To join strips, position two strips at right angles to each other, right sides facing and their raw edges meeting. Overlap the pieces of fabric so that the corners extend on either side and you can stitch by machine from edge to edge and 12mm (½in) from the raw ends.

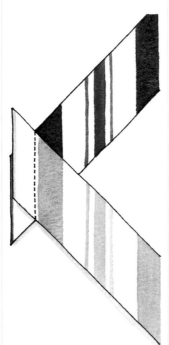

4. Lay the long strip of binding in front of you, wrong side uppermost. Press all the joining seams open and trim away the corners which are still protruding.

5. Place the piping cord on top then fold the long strip of fabric lengthways over the cord, until its raw edges meet. Pin all the way along the strip, as close as possible to the cord, securing it in place.

6. Attach the pinned covered piping cord to the right side of one of the squares of ticking, pinning it around the four sides of the ticking square so that the raw edges of the piping covering align with the raw edges of the ticking and the corded edge faces inwards towards the middle of the fabric square.

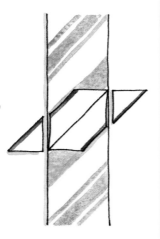

7. Using a piping foot on the sewing machine, adjusted so that the needle is between the foot and the piping cord, carefully machine stitch close to the cord, but avoid sewing through it. Remove the pins as you work.

8. Lay the second square of fabric on top of the first, right sides facing. Pin and baste in place, leaving one side of the square open for inserting the cushion pad.

9. Machine stitch carefully around three sides of the cushion cover, again taking care not to catch the piping cord in the seam at any point.

10. Turn the cover the right side out; turn in and press the seam allowance along the cushion cover opening. Insert the cushion pad. Pin then sew the opening closed with small neat hand stitches.

PLEATED-EDGE CUSHION – 2 HOURS

You will need

Sharp scissors
Tape measure
0.5m (½yd) striped ticking
Remnant of heavyweight soft white linen for edging
Long glass-headed pins
Sewing machine / needle and white thread
33cm (13in) square cushion pad

This ancient navy-and-white ticking was a gift from a good friend who is a textile dealer. Quite a lot of it was holed and badly marked with rust and had to be discarded. There are a few rust marks on the cushions but they do not detract from the cushions' crisp freshness. The pleated edge of the cushions is made up from a lovely old linen sheet, which had been ripped in half to save the best part. It had been well patched and repaired over the years and this has been made a feature. I particularly love the softness of the rather faded, well-washed appearance of something old and well cared for.

1. Cut out two 35.5cm (14in) squares of striped ticking.

2. Cut out two or three strips of soft white linen, 12.5cm (5in) wide. Cut them from selvage to selvage if possible, otherwise you

will have to neaten the raw ends of the strips by turning them in twice neatly then stitching by machine or hand.

3. Fold the strips in half lengthways, right sides facing outwards, and press.

4. Take a strip and pin it to the right side of one of the squares of fabric, pleating it evenly as shown, the raw edges together and the long folded edge of the strip towards the middle of the square of fabric. If you come across an old patch that someone has taken the trouble to repair – perhaps a hundred years ago – don't hide it but highlight it by making the pleat larger.

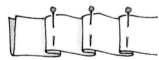

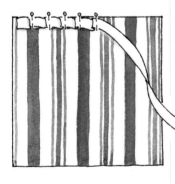

5. When you reach the end of the strip, overlap it with the end of a new strip and continue pleating in the same direction as before. Alternatively, fold back the end and begin the next strip by folding it back in the opposite direction, as illustrated.

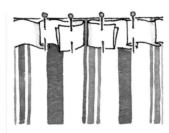

6. When you have edged the entire square of fabric, make any necessary adjustments so that the pleats are roughly the same size – except those that are patched. Baste the pleated edging in place before machine stitching, allowing at least a 2cm (³⁄₄in) seam.

7. Before completing the cushion cover, fold in the pleated edging strip at each corner towards the middle of the fabric square and secure temporarily with a pin well away from the seam line to avoid any possibility of damaging the sewing machine needle.

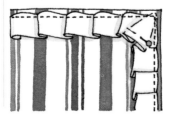

8. Lay the second square of ticking on top of the edged square, right sides facing. Pin

then machine stitch together, taking care on the pinned corners. Leave one side of the square open for inserting the cushion pad.

9. Turn the cover the right side out, then turn in and press the seam allowance along the cushion cover opening. Insert the cushion pad. Pin then sew the opening closed with small neat hand stitches.

SUMMER-TIME BLUES

These cushions are further examples of Pleated-Edge Cushions, but the pleated trimming used here is made from a remnant of cotton that has been dyed by hand. Cotton fabric can be easily dyed in an old saucepan if it is only a small amount – follow the directions on the product. Lovely effects can be achieved quite by accident, for example unusual markings forming where the fabric was creased in the pan. Rinse the fabric thoroughly after dyeing and leave to dry, before pressing it well.

French chair

This pretty chair, in desperate need of stripping, respringing and re-covering, was purchased at a French antiques fair. Once stripped of paint, it was professionally resprung and restuffed in the traditional way, just as it would have been a hundred years ago. It was then updated with navy-and-white ticking with a simple trim and given a gentle touch of chalky emulsion paint.

1 HOUR

You will need

Heavy-duty rubber gloves
Craftsman's paint stripper
Scraper with renewable blades
Stripping knife
100 grade and finer sandpaper
Polythene
Narrow fitch or 12mm–2cm (½–¾in) household brush
Small quantity (tester pot) of a vinyl-free, water-based, chalky emulsion paint
Kitchen paper

Unless you are good at upholstery yourself, re-covering a chair like this one is not a simple task. The hard, squared-off shield-shaped sprung back is the problem. It is wiser to have such chairs covered professionally by a recommended upholsterer. If your chair has loose joints or is damaged, a good upholsterer will carry out the repairs for you, or pass the work on to an antique dealer if it is beyond his or her capabilities. All good upholsterers are insured. The upholsterer will have a wide range of fabric for

you to choose from if you do not wish to supply your own.

1. The first step is to strip the chair of unwanted layers of paint. Making sure that you wear heavy-duty gloves and take the appropriate safety precautions, apply the paint stripper carefully following the manufacturer's instructions. Use a scraper and stripping knife and take particular care around the carved areas of the chair.

2. Once the chair has been stripped and allowed to dry out, sand the wood, always working in the same direction as the grain. Begin with 100 grade sandpaper then move on to the finer sandpaper to finish.

3. Upholster the chair yourself or have it done for you by a recommended upholsterer.

4. Once the chair has been upholstered the wooden frame can be painted, but first cover the new upholstery extremely carefully with polythene in order to protect it. Using an almost dry paintbrush and very little paint,

very carefully brush a little vinyl-free emulsion paint over the wood. Apply paint to the raised surfaces in particular – the carving and reeded legs – allowing the original wood to

show through. Leave the paint to dry before applying a second coat, again very sparingly, and using kitchen paper to wipe away excess paint.

Monogrammed linen armchair cover

This is an easy way to bring a crisp, clean look of summery freshness to a sitting room. These beautiful ecru-coloured antique heavyweight linen sheets lighten up the room to give an airy, almost Mediterranean feel; their red embroidered monograms are an added bonus.

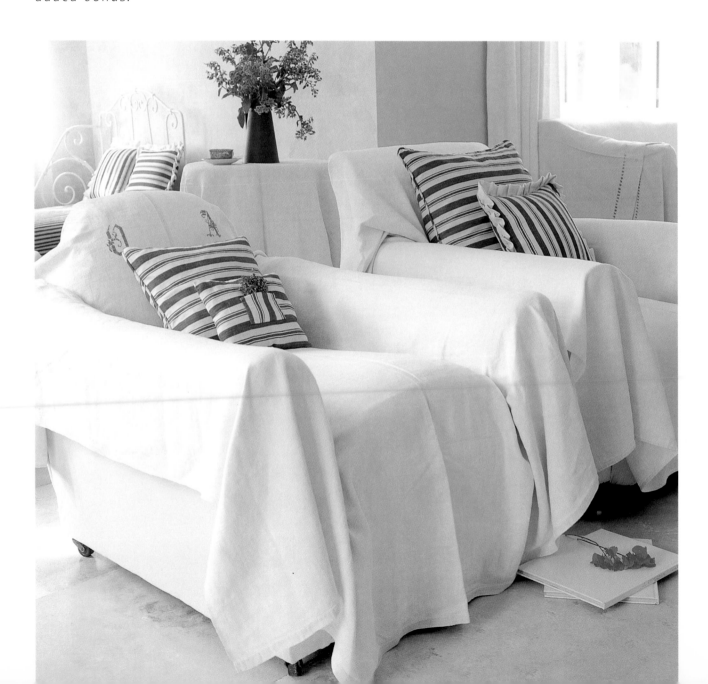

HALF AN HOUR

You will need

*Heavyweight linen double sheet
(monogrammed if you wish)
Armchair*

Unlike loose covers, which are exceptionally awkward to iron and take a good deal of pulling and pushing of over-tight fabric to get them to fit over furniture, these lovely old sheets take only a minute or two to put in place. When a cover becomes too creased or dirty it can be whipped off and replaced with another one. Such heavyweight linen sheets not only launder wonderfully or dry quickly on a clothes line in wind or sun, they also iron very well. For the best results, keep a fine spray bottle filled with lavender water by the ironing board to dampen the linen as you iron.

1. Hold up the sheet with the hemmed edges top and bottom and the loom seam running vertically down the middle. Place the sheet over the armchair with

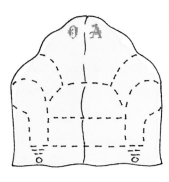

the loom seam in the middle of the chair back and the monogrammed initials towards the top where they can be seen.

2. Stand behind the chair and adjust the sheet until the hem is level with the bottom edge of the chair at the back.

3. Now work from in front of the chair and lift the excess sheet that will be on the floor at the front until it, too, is level with the bottom edge of the front of the chair. Smooth the sheet from the front to the back of the seat and down the chair back below the monograms. Tuck the excess in deeply behind the seat cushion.

4. Next tuck in the sheet at the sides deeply, keeping the central loom seam in the middle of the seat. This will bring the sheet up from the floor on the outside of the arms thereby revealing some of the chair.

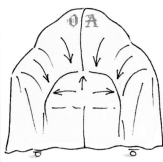

5. Now tuck in the excess amounts of sheet as far back as possible at the points where the backs of the arms meet the chair back. Make a deep fold or pleat in

each of these two corners so that the fabric lies flat on the actual chair arms.

6. Finally, pick up the two corners of the sheet behind the chair and make a lovely big knot across the back of the chair.

Toile de Jouy curtains

Blue and white is an almost foolproof colour combination; light and fresh, it is perfect for summer and winter alike. Here, a wide border and overhanging top in a lovely pale blue toile de Jouy introduce a touch of colour to plain white floor-length curtains made from fine antique French linen sheets.

A WEEKEND

You will need

*2 white antique French linen double
    sheets*
Tape measure
Long glass-headed pins
*Length of toile de Jouy, 137cm (54in)
    wide*
*Straight edge and light pencil
    (optional)*
Sharp scissors
Sewing machine
Needle and white thread

The French linen sheets have been used upside-down to show off their beautiful drawn thread work and white embroidery – which would normally be turned over the top of the bed quilt – at the foot of the curtains.

If your windows are very large you may wish to adjust the amount of overhang as 30cm (12in) may not look sufficient. The sheets used here measure 218 x 310cm (86 x 122in) and required 5m (5½yd) toile. You would need about 6.5m (7yd) toile to match the pattern on the overhanging top to that of the curtain edge beneath. If you need to adjust the length of the sheets

to suit your windows remove any excess fabric from the plain, undecorated end of each sheet before beginning the project.

1. Lay one sheet on a large work surface, using it so that the plain, undecorated end will be at the top of the curtain. To work out the length of the toile required for the side borders, first measure then use pins to mark a line 30cm (12in) down from the top edge of the sheet and parallel to it. Next, measure from the line of pins down the length of the curtain (left-hand curtain illustrated here) to the decorative hem where the toile side border will end. Add 2.5cm (1in) top and bottom to allow for turning under the toile raw edges.

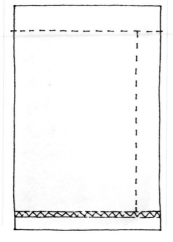

2. Unroll the length of toile on the work surface. Using pins, mark out the required length of the side border, as determined in Step 1. Using more pins or a straight edge and a light pencil, mark a cutting line 35.5cm (14in) away from the left-hand edge, and parallel to it. Using this cutting line, cut out the border for the left-hand curtain.

3. Cut out the second border in exactly the same way. Lightly pencil distinguishing marks on the back of each strip of toile so that you remember which is for the left-hand curtain and which for the right, so the pattern on the two borders will match up when the curtains are drawn.

Press under a 2.5cm (1in) turning at the top and bottom of each border piece.

4. Lay the sheet for the left-hand curtain on the work surface once more, with the wrong side (the back of the sheet) facing upwards. Lay the toile border, also wrong side uppermost, on the sheet, aligning the long edges and positioning the neatened top edge of the border against the marked 30cm (12in) guideline. Pin the toile strip to the sheet along the long edge. Machine stitch. Press the seam flat.

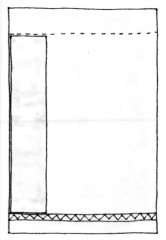

5. Bring the toile border around to the right side of the sheet (the front of the curtain), then press under the long raw edge. Pin the border to the sheet all round, then hand sew with tiny 'invisible' stitches. Attach the other border to the right-hand curtain in the same way.

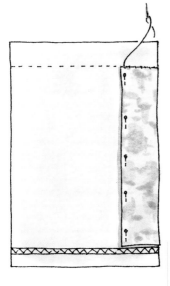

6. Cut four widths of toile, 35.5cm (14in) deep, for the overhanging curtain tops. If you have sufficient fabric try to match the pattern in the toile when cutting out these pieces – where the overhanging top lies against the curtain side border, and also where the two widths per curtain for the overhanging tops are joined together. However, any pattern difference is unlikely to be noticed if the colours are pale, as here, and the joining seam in the overhanging top will probably be hidden in the folds of the curtain even when the curtains are drawn.

7. For each curtain, pin then machine stitch two widths together, right sides facing, to make one long strip for the overhanging top, matching the pattern if possible.

8. Lay one curtain on the work surface, wrong side uppermost. Measure then use pins to mark a guideline 33cm (13in) down from the top edge of the sheet and parallel to it. Lay a long strip of toile across the sheet, wrong side uppermost. Pin one long edge to the sheet along the 33cm (13in) guideline, allowing the short ends to overlap the sheet slightly. Machine stitch in place. Press the seam flat.

9. Bring the toile 'flap' up over the seam so that the right side of the toile is now uppermost and

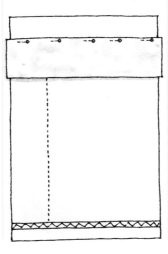

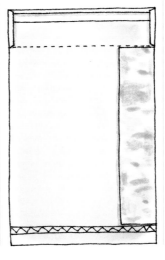

covering the top of the sheet. Turn the toile's raw edges in twice over the edges of the sheet to neaten; machine stitch.

10. Turn the toile top over to the front of the sheet to overhang the curtain. The seam line joining the toile to the sheet and along which the toile is folded over to the front now becomes the top edge of the curtain.

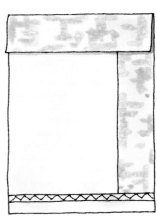

Toile de Jouy lampshades

These two pretty little lampshades were made from the leftover fabric from the toile de Jouy curtains (see page 58); even the trims are handmade. The two candlestick lamp bases were a dark mahogany colour and purchased at a knock-down price. Painted white, they look completely different!

A WEEKEND

You will need

*Small, shaped lampshade
     frame, 15cm (6in) diameter
     at the top and 20cm (8in)
     diameter at the base*
Sharp scissors
Cotton lampshade tape
Long glass-headed pins
Needle and matching thread
Thimble
Remnant of toile de Jouy
*Clear fabric glue or hot glue
     gun and glue stick*

Lampshade frames need binding with cotton tape to cover roughly cut wire joints, which would eventually damage the fabric; the tape also provides a base on which to sew. Start by binding the upright struts of the frame; some people bind only the two side struts, I prefer to bind them all and it is much easier to secure the fabric later on if you bind the whole frame. It is advisable to wear a thimble when sewing through the tape to prevent pushing the blunt end of the needle into your finger or under your nail, which is very painful!

1. Take the lampshade frame and cut a length of cotton tape for each side strut – about 2½ times the length of each strut. Prepare to start binding at the top of one strut. To secure the tape, hold the end of the tape near the top of the upright, then wrap the tape around the junction where the upright meets the top ring in a figure of eight, as illustrated. Continue by working downwards, pulling the tape tightly at an angle around the strut and overlapping the tape each time by about a third. Always keep a tension on the tape otherwise it will unfurl and you will have to begin again.

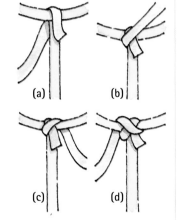

(a)   (b)

(c)   (d)

2. When you reach the bottom of the first strut, make another figure of eight in the same way as before. Push a pin deep into the tape to secure it while you cut off the excess tape. Turn under the raw end and secure to the binding with a few stitches.

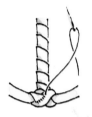

3. Bind the rest of the side struts in the same way.

4. To bind the top and bottom rings of the frame, cut a length of tape approximately three times the circumference of each ring. Bind the rings just as before – starting and finishing with figures of eight, keeping tension on the tape as you work and winding figures of eight around the frame each time you come to a side strut. As before, no stitching should be required to secure the tape at the starting point if you do it properly.

5. You now need to cut two pieces of toile for the lampshade, selecting the design to fit the frame appropriately. Lay the frame on its side on the fabric and cut out the fabric around the frame, allowing an extra 5cm (2in) above the top and at the sides of the frame and an extra 7.5cm (3in) at the bottom. This gives you fabric to hold on to while pulling it tight to pin it to the frame. Cut a second piece of fabric the same size.

6. Lay the frame on its side and lay one of the pieces of toile on the uppermost half of the frame. Push a few pins into the side strut binding at either side until the fabric is taut, but not too much. Readjust the pins as you work to eradicate any unevenness or loose areas.

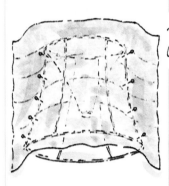

7. Start to pull the fabric at the bottom of the frame next, remembering that the tension is pulled on the cross: if you pull the toile at the bottom right it will affect the top left, and so on. Secure the fabric with pins pushed through the binding tape as before.

8. Lastly, pull the fabric at the top of the frame and insert more pins. When the whole area of fabric is taut and straight, check the pins near the bottom of the side struts again and readjust if necessary. When you are satisfied, begin to stitch the fabric to the bound frame with very small, firm stitches on the outside of the frame. Do not remove a pin until the area beneath it has been stitched. Use the plump areas of tape in the figure of eights at the top and bottom of each strut to sew deeply and firmly.

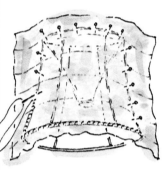

9. Cover the other half of the lampshade frame with the second piece of toile in exactly the same way.

10. When both pieces of fabric are stitched down all round, trim the toile at the top and bottom of the frame to no less than 12mm (½in). Fold this 12mm (½in) of excess fabric back; if the fabric is too taut to turn back, make tiny cuts along the edge. Using a long blanket stitch, sew through this layer of turned-back fabric to secure it loosely to the bound frame. Trim the fabric closer to the stitching. (The raw edges of fabric and the stitching will eventually be concealed beneath the trimming.)

11. Trim the excess fabric at the sides of the frame where the two pieces of toile meet, cutting close to the stitching.

12. To make the self-trimming for the two side struts of the lampshade where the two pieces of toile meet, cut two 2cm (¾in) wide strips of fabric to the required length, allowing a little extra for turning under the raw ends. Cut a strip to trim the top edge of the lampshade similarly. Fold the three strips in half lengthways, right sides facing outwards, then turn their long raw edges into the middle and press. Turn under their short ends and secure with 'invisible' stitches or a tiny blob of glue.

13. Clear fabric glue is the easiest way to attach the self-trimming to the lampshade – you can anchor the strips at each end with pins stuck into the bound frame while the glue sets.

However, you cannot use securing pins if you use a hot glue gun as the glue sets too quickly and will trap the pins. Align the neatened ends of each side trimming strip with the top and bottom of the lampshade and glue the two lengths of trimming in place. Take care not to drip any glue on the lampshade fabric as you work.

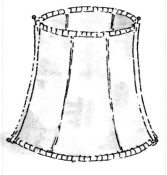

14. To trim the top edge, glue one neatened end of the trimming near one of the trimmed side 'seams'. Continue gluing the trimming in place around the top edge of the lampshade. Finish with the remaining neatened end butted up accurately against the first.

15. To make the trimming for the bottom edge of the lampshade, cut several strips of fabric, 3cm (1¼in) wide. Stitch them together, right sides facing, to make one very long strip. Press the seams open. Press the long raw edges under and then towards each other to meet in the centre. Slipstitch these edges together – this will be the back of the trimming.

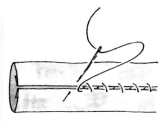

16. To make the bows, start a little way from one end of the strip and make a fold as illustrated (a); make another fold of equal depth (b), then a third fold (c). Sew the folds together with a few central stitches through all layers of fabric (d).

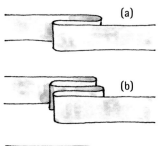

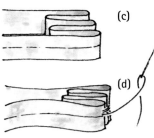

17. Open out the stitched folded fabric to reveal the beginnings of a bow.

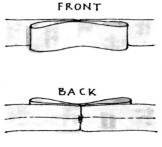

18. Thread a needle and knot one end of the thread. Pass the needle from the back of the strip to the folded front and secure the thread well with a few tiny stitches. Sew tiny running stitches across the centre of the folded fabric.

19. Draw the fabric along the thread to gather it into a bow shape. Push the needle through to the back and fasten off the thread securely with several more stitches.

20. Continue making bows in this way at evenly spaced intervals along the strip of fabric. When you have completed the trimming place one raw end of the strip just beyond the side 'seam' and against the bottom edge of the lampshade. Secure with a pin and run the trimming around the shade to check the length is sufficient. Remove the pin; heat the glue gun then glue the trimming in position, working gradually around the lampshade. When you reach the point at which you began, turn under the remaining end of the trimming and secure with a tiny blob of glue. Glue it down, overlapping the raw end already in place.

Linen sofa cover with ties

Would you like to change the look of your sitting room for the summer months without having to change the furniture? For the price of two antique linen sheets, fabric in cheerful summery colours to make cushions and a small eye-catching quilt you can achieve an entirely new country-style transformation.

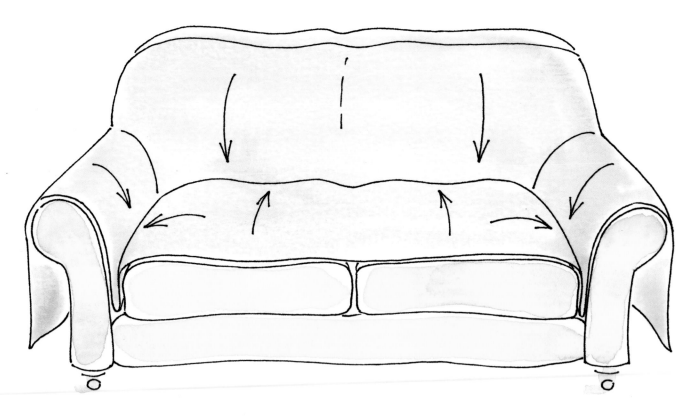

2 HOURS

You will need

2 ecru or off-white antique
    European heavyweight linen
    double sheets
Sofa to be covered
Sharp scissors
Remnant of linen to make the ties

Tape measure
Long glass-headed pins
Sewing machine (optional)
Needle and matching thread
Quilt and cushions

If you already own an old quilt so much the better; if not, visit an antiques fair for a fascinating and fun day out – you may well find other tempting bargains! There are several ways to cover a sofa using two sheets – experiment to find the style that best suits your sofa.

1. Open out the first sheet and drape it evenly over the sofa with the central loom seam running from one end of the sofa to the other. Stand behind the sofa and ensure the edge of the sheet is level with the bottom edge of the sofa at the back.

2. Tuck in about 30cm (12in) deeply down the back of the sofa, behind the seat cushions, and the same amount at the sides of the

cushions and at the back of the arms if appropriate. After making the tucks there should be sufficient fabric left to cover the top of the seat cushions and the arms and to hang down over the sides of the sofa.

3. Open out the second sheet ready to use lengthways this time, so that its central seam runs from the back to the front of the sofa. Fold under the edges as necessary so that the sheet fits the width of your sofa, inside the arms. Position the sheet centrally over the sofa back. Working from the front, align the sheet with the front bottom edge of the sofa, almost on the floor, smooth it over the seat, then tuck it down a little way behind the seat cushions. This may bring the end of the sheet at the back of the sofa up from the ground, but this is not important as the first sheet covers the sofa back already.

4. To make the ties, cut four strips of old linen, 15 x 92cm (6 x 36in). Turn under the raw edges on each strip, then fold in half lengthways, right sides facing outwards, and press. On each strip, pin then machine topstitch around the three sides, close to the edge, or sew by hand.

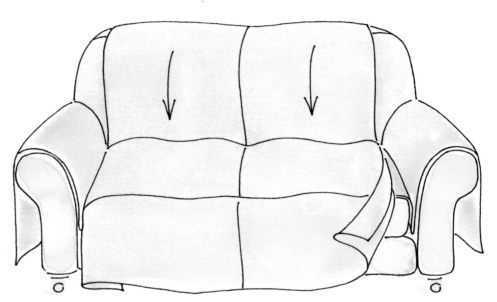

5. Tuck this linen sheet into deep folds at the back and sides of the sofa until it hangs perfectly. Pin two ties in position each side of the sofa to hold the folded sheet in place, as well as to create an attractive detail.

6. Sew the ties to the sheet by hand, securing them firmly with neat stitches. Tie them into attractive floppy bows.

7. Throw a quilt over the back of the sofa, add colourful cushions and relax in sumptuously comfortable country style.

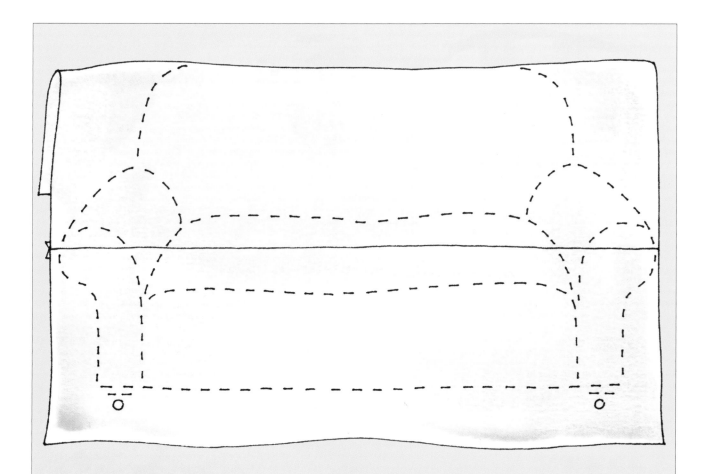

ALTERNATIVE PLACING OF SHEETS

1. Drape the first sheet over the sofa and tuck it in as described above (see steps 1 and 2).

2. Open out the second sheet ready to use it over the sofa in the same direction as the first sheet, i.e. with the loom seam running the length of the sofa. Fold under almost a quarter of the width of the sheet – the amount will depend on the depth of your sofa and can be adjusted to suit. The folded-under fabric will be tucked down the back of the sofa. The loom seam should be still visible running across the seat near the back of the sofa, in front of the back cushions.

3. Working from the front, lay the sheet over the sofa, then tuck in the folded-under section so that the edge of the sheet at the front of the sofa is level with the sofa's bottom front edge, almost on the floor. Next, tuck the sheet in at the back, behind the arms and at the sides. The hemmed ends of the sheet should end up level with the bottom side edges of the sofa, just above the floor. This method totally covers the sides of the sofa underneath.

4. Continue as described above (see Steps 4–7), tucking the linen sheet into deep folds until it hangs perfectly and making and attaching ties to the sheet, to tie into floppy bows.

Canvas ticking bolster

Simple and quick to make, blissfully comfortable and multi-purpose, these hard-wearing, washable canvas ticking bolsters are great for using on a sunbed or in a garden hammock, and can double up as extra pillows for overnight guests. Each bolster is made with a hard-wearing French seam then filled with the softest laundered single eiderdown, which is simply rolled up, or could be stuffed into a kit-bag or bolster case first.

I HOUR

You will need

Sharp scissors
Tape measure
1m (1¼yd) canvas ticking, 140cm (55in) wide
Long glass-headed pins
Sewing machine
Matching thread
Old clean single eiderdown
1.5m (1¾yd) soft rope

1. Cut a 94 x 140cm (37 x 54in) rectangle of ticking.

2. For the French seam, pin the long raw-edged sides of the rectangle together, right sides facing outwards, to make a tube shape, taking a 1.5cm (⅝in) seam allowance. Machine stitch.

3. Trim the seam allowances and press together. Turn the bolster cover inside out, so that the right side of the fabric is

inside the 'tube', folding the fabric along the line of stitching. Pin then machine stitch parallel with this seam and 2cm (¾in) away from it, to enclose the raw edges of the first seam.

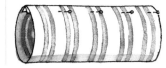

4. Turn under the selvages by about 2cm (¾in) at both ends of the bolster. Pin then machine stitch. Turn the bolster back to the right side.

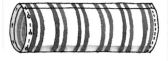

5. Stuff the middle of the bolster with a rolled-up single eiderdown, leaving excess fabric each end of the bolster.

6. Cut the rope into two 75cm (30in) lengths and knot each end. To hold the eiderdown in place within the bolster cover, tie a length of rope around each end of the bolster like a cracker, and secure with a knot.

Gingham-covered eiderdown

Gingham has a timeless charm; always crisp and fresh, it looks good in any room and combines well with other checks and with floral designs. Here, an old eiderdown has been re-covered with gingham for a fresh country look.

A MORNING

You will need

Tape measure
Eiderdown to be covered
Length of gingham fabric, at least 115cm (44–45in) wide
Heavy white antique linen sheet
Sharp scissors
Long glass-headed pins
Sewing machine
Needle and red thread

Authentic eiderdowns have made a comeback and fit well with the new country-style look. Once the poor relation of the quilt, they are lighter, warmer and a great deal cheaper! Look out for old eiderdowns in antique markets or car boot sales. An eiderdown for sale may be displayed rolled up and tied attractively. If so, open it out and turn it over to check for immovable stains and holes, which will affect the price you may wish to pay. To freshen an old eiderdown after years of storage, mend any holes, machine wash and tumble dry it several times as the down or feathers hold water and must be dried.

The 1960s-style man-made equivalents of authentic eiderdowns can be re-covered in just the same way.

Good alternatives to gingham include the modern floral fabrics with a faded appearance, which are perfect for this project.

1. To calculate the amount of gingham you will need, measure the length and width of the eiderdown and add 5cm (2in) all round for the seams. (You may need to allow a little more, depending on the 'puffiness' of the down.) Also ensure there will be sufficient remnants to cut strips for the trimming.

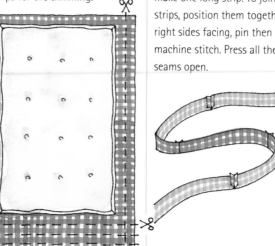

2. Using the measurements determined in Step 1, cut out two pieces of fabric for the main body of the eiderdown cover – cut one piece from gingham and another piece from the white linen sheet.

3. For the eiderdown's frilly edges, cut long strips of fabric, 5cm (2in) wide, from the remaining gingham. You need enough strips such that, when joined together and with the fabric slightly gathered, they can edge the large panel of gingham.

4. Join all the narrow strips of gingham together, end to end, to make one long strip. To join the strips, position them together, right sides facing, pin then machine stitch. Press all the seams open.

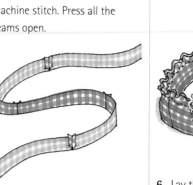

5. Fold the strip in half lengthways, right side facing outwards, and press. Using thread doubled for strength, secure the thread well by oversewing a few stitches then sew the long edges of the gingham together using a loose running stitch. Draw the fabric along the thread to gather it. Before the thread becomes too short, cut it off and secure the loose ends of thread temporarily by wrapping them several times in a figure of eight around a glass-headed pin stuck in the fabric. Continue in the same way until the edging is gathered to the required length.

6. Lay the large panel of gingham, right side uppermost, on your work surface. Pin the gathered edging around the edge of the gingham panel, their raw edges meeting. Ease the gathered edging evenly all the way round, making adjustments where necessary. Baste then machine stitch slowly and carefully, removing the odd pin securing the ends of gathering threads when you come to it. Once the edging has been stitched in place, pull out the gathering stitches where possible.

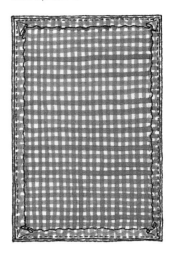

7. With right sides facing, lay the panel of white linen on top of the edged gingham panel. Pin then machine stitch around three sides of the cover only, leaving one short end open through which to insert the eiderdown.

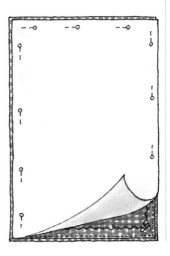

8. Turn the fabric the right side out and press if necessary. Insert the eiderdown inside the cover. Turn in the seam allowances, pin the ends together then hand stitch neatly in place.

9. The last step is to secure the eiderdown to its new cover – you will need to pin then baste the layers before stitching. It may be possible to follow the original stitched pattern of the old eiderdown if it is not too complicated. If it is difficult to

machine stitch through the eiderdown, hand sewing may be more viable. Working from the front and using red thread doubled for strength, use a long running stitch in a simple design to sew through from one side to the other. Check the back frequently to ensure the stitches are in a straight line. If this proves unworkable, simply secure the eiderdown in two places in the middle of the eiderdown, and approximately 25cm (10in) in from each corner.

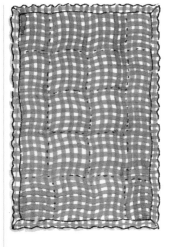

Ricrac-trimmed cushions

Ricrac is hot news again and back in style for interiors. It is easy to use and effective for brightening up plain fabric such as the white linen used for these simple cushions. Each cushion is made with one piece of fabric, wrapped over and fastened with buttons. The attractively finished cushion back can so easily become the front of the cushion, fastened with decorative 1940s-style or fabric-covered buttons.

2 HOURS

You will need

Sharp scissors
Length of white linen, old or new
Tape measure
Long glass-headed pins
Sewing machine
Needle, white and red thread
Length of red ricrac
3–4 buttons
35.5cm (14in) square cushion pad

A remnant of white cotton or linen or part of an old linen sheet would be ideal for these stylish cushions. Ricrac is available from ribbon shops or the haberdashery departments of large stores.

The buttonholes in this project are made at the end when the cushion cover is complete and it is easier to see where to position them. However, it is more fiddly so you might prefer to make your buttonholes after Step 1. You will, however, have to take care positioning them at this stage, remembering to allow for the turnings top and bottom and the 5cm (2in) border around the cushion pad.

If you allow for a larger overlap – about 7.5–10cm (3–4in) – at the back of the cushion cover, the cushion pad will stay in place without buttons at all.

1. Cut out a rectangle of white linen, 88.5 x 48cm (35 x 19in). Turn under 2.5cm (1in) of fabric on the short ends of the rectangle, pin and machine stitch.

2. Lay the rectangle of fabric vertically on the work surface in front of you, as shown, right side uppermost. Fold the top section of the fabric over to the middle of the rectangle.

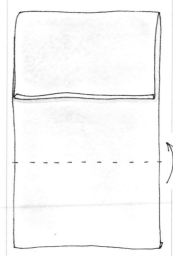

3. Now fold the bottom section to the middle, overlapping the first piece by 2.5cm (1in). Pin then machine stitch the two sides of the cushion cover together using white thread, 12mm (½in) away from the raw edges. Press,

turn the cushion cover to the right side and then press flat.

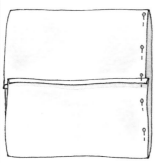

4. Measure 5cm (2in) in from the edges of the cushion cover and pin the two layers together all the way round. Machine stitch using white thread along the line of pins, removing them as you work.

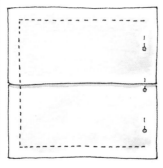

5. Pin the ricrac around the cushion cover on top of the line you have just stitched. Start at one corner and begin by turning under one end of the ricrac two or three times, then securing it with a few stitches to prevent fraying. Using red thread, machine topstitch the ricrac in place. When you have stitched all around the cover, make a loop where the two ends of ricrac meet. Turn under the second end of ricrac as before and secure.

6. Make three or four buttonholes along the edge of the overlapping fabric on the cushion cover back. Sew the buttons in place on the underlap, aligning them accurately with the buttonholes you have made. Insert the cushion pad and do up the buttons.

Voile slipcover

The prettily shaped, painted wooden chair is dressed in a tightly bodiced 'gown' and full skirt of white cotton voile for a soft, feminine look.

1. Lay a length of voile over the chair, from below the front edge of the seat to below the seat at the back, allowing an overhang all round of at least 10cm (4in).

2. Pin together the voile hanging over the chair back, following the shape all the way round. Start putting some tension on the voile, repositioning the pins closer and closer to the chair back each time until the voile is a tight fit.

3. Hand sew with the neatest backstitches possible, pushing the needle first from one side, then to the other, all the time keeping some tension on the fabric. Sew as close to the wood as possible. Remove the pins as you work. When you have finished stitching, use sharp scissors to trim away the excess voile close to the stitches.

4. Lift the chair on to a table or work surface and tip it forwards so that you can work more easily on the underside of the chair seat. Pull the voile tightly to fit across the seat, smoothing out any creases. Turn under the raw edges and staple the voile at intervals to the underside of the chair seat, all the way round.

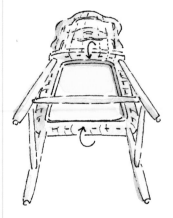

5. Measure the distance from the chair seat to the ground to determine the length of the voile skirt required, adding an extra 6.5cm (2½in) to allow for

A MORNING

You will need

Length of white cotton voile, 165cm (65in) wide

Chair to be covered

Tape measure

Long glass-headed pins
Needle and white thread
Sharp scissors
Staple gun and staples
Sewing machine
Safety pin
2.5m (2¾yd) fine white ribbon

turnings. Cut 1½–2 full widths of voile to this measurement to make the skirt.

6. Join the side edges of the fabric panels together to make one long panel, using French seams (see Steps 2–3, Country Dressing Table with Gathered Skirt, page 75).

7. Turn the two short ends of the skirt panel under twice, pin and machine stitch.

8. Turn under 4cm (1½in) along the top edge of the skirt panel and turn under 2.5cm (1in) for the hem. Pin and machine stitch. Attach a safety pin to one end of the fine ribbon and thread it through the casing created at the top of the skirt, gathering the voile evenly along the ribbon.

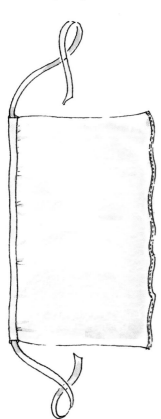

9. Secure one end of the skirt with pins into the seat fabric just in front of one of the back legs. Wrap the skirt around the chair, holding it in place with pins as you work your way round, until you reach your starting point.

10. Tie the ends of the ribbon together tightly and secure with a pin. Attach the top of the skirt to the chair seat fabric by hand stitching around the seat, making sure the skirt is gathered evenly all the way round.

ROSE-DECORATED LAMPSHADE

To decorate a plain fabric lampshade to complement this slipcover, find a printed fabric with an appealing design, such as a group of beautiful full-blown roses. Cut out the piece of fabric roughly. Mix about 2 tablespoons PVA adhesive with 1 litre (1¾ pints) water in a bowl. Place the fabric in the solution and stir it well to ensure it becomes well saturated. Remove from the bowl and hang on a line or spread out on an old clean towel to dry.

Iron the piece of fabric flat while still a little damp. It should be quite stiff now and perfect for cutting out accurately.

Attach the motif to a plain fabric lampshade – to the slipcover, too, if liked – using a clear fabric glue, or use it as a motif for appliqué work and attach with tiny neat hand stitches.

Linen scrim slipcover

Huge lacy white hydrangea heads make a wonderful backdrop for this white linen scrim slipcover trimmed with beautiful heavy antique lace. The cover was made to prettify an otherwise rather plain old iron fairground chair that can be used outside in the garden during the summer months.

2 HOURS

You will need

Tape measure
Chair to be covered
Sharp scissors
Length of natural linen scrim
Long glass-headed pins
Sewing machine
Length of heavy antique lace,
*   10–12.5cm (4–5in) deep*
Needle and white thread

The openly woven texture of the scrim looks airy and light making it an ideal project for a bedroom. Simple, white full-length curtains or a lace-trimmed blind made from the same material would create an inexpensive and unusual scheme.

1. Measure from the level of the seat at the back of the chair, up over the chair back, down the front of the chair back and over the seat to overhang the front edge of the seat by about 15cm (6in). Measure the width of the chair and add a seam allowance of 2.5cm (1in) all round. Cut out a rectangle to these measurements from the linen scrim and lay the fabric over the chair, wrong side uppermost.

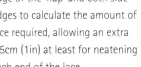

2. Down the sides of the chair pin together the fabric that hangs over the chair back. Remove the fabric from the chair and machine stitch along the pinned seams.

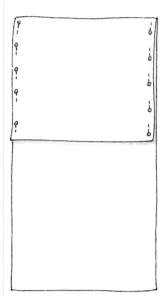

3. Turn the fabric the right side out and press. Turn under all the remaining raw edges twice to neaten and prevent fraying. Pin then machine stitch.

4. Measure the back bottom edge of the 'flap' and both side edges to calculate the amount of lace required, allowing an extra 2.5cm (1in) at least for neatening each end of the lace.

5. Pin the lace to the slipcover, turning in the raw ends of the lace neatly and securely to prevent fraying. Machine or hand stitch the lace trimming in place. Press the cover, then slip it in place over the chair back.

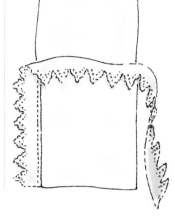

Patched bedspread

New vintage-style fabrics with authentic-looking faded roses and buds bring a touch of nostalgia to this 1940s-style bedroom. Those used for the patched bedspread, rose-trimmed lampshade and rosebud cushion mix well with the original 1940s eiderdown and fabric-covered box. The top sheet and pillowcase are made from a huge, 19th-century hand-woven tablecloth from Alsace.

front

reverse

A DAY

You will need

Sharp scissors
2m (2¼yd) each of three different
    rose designs in cotton, 140cm
    (55in) wide
Long glass-headed pins
Sewing machine
Heavy white cotton single
    bedspread, or part of one,

measuring 170 x 185cm
    (67 x 73in)
Tape measure
Needle and matching thread

It is easy to replicate the look and style of the 1940s era with the pretty, faded-looking floral prints being produced today. The basis for this project was part of an old heavy white cotton bedspread, its worn edges cut off, which gives

body and weight to the patchwork front and adds credence to the bedspread being in vintage style.

The patchwork front is made up from seven large pieces of three different rose designs (labelled 1, 2 and 3) – two faded-looking fabrics and one modern print. It is backed by the old bedspread remnant, itself decorated with a patch of floral fabric. Strips on the side edges of

the patchwork panel fold over to the underside of the bedspread to edge both the front and back of the bedspread. Narrower strips edge the top and bottom edges of the bedspread similarly.

You may be fortunate enough to find suitable old fabric from a mature family member who may have curtains tucked away. Otherwise try an antique market, jumble sale or charity shop.

1. First make the patchwork front. Cut out two strips from Fabric 1, each measuring 41 x 185cm (16 x 73in).

2. From Fabric 2 cut out two strips, 33 x 185cm (13 x 73in), and one rectangular piece, 74 x 104cm (29 x 41in).

3. Cut two rectangles from Fabric 3, each measuring 43 x 74cm (17 x 29in). In addition, cut two long strips from Fabric 3, each measuring 18 x 173cm (7 x 68¼in), for the top and bottom edges of the bedspread.

4. To make up the sides of the patchwork front, place a strip of Fabric 1 and Fabric 2 together, right sides facing. Pin then machine stitch along one long edge. Repeat with second pair.

5. To make the central vertical panel of the patchwork front, place the rectangle of Fabric 2 on a work surface, right side uppermost. To each of the shorter sides (the top and bottom edges) of this rectangle, pin a long side of a Fabric 3 rectangle, right sides facing. Machine stitch.

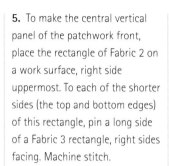

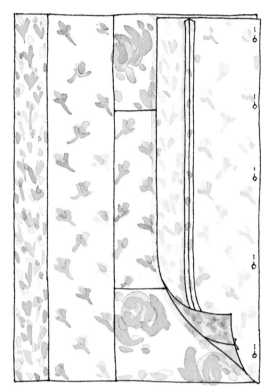

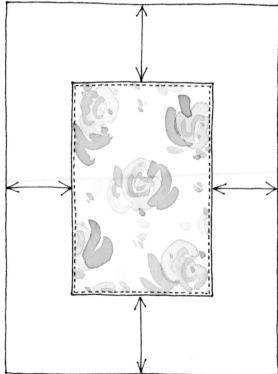

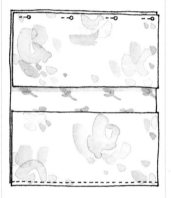

6. Open out all the pieces you have just stitched and press the seams open. You now have the three main sections for the patchwork front of the bedspread, which are ready to be joined together. Pin one long edge of each side piece to the central section, right sides facing. Machine stitch. Open out and press all the seams open.

7. To decorate the underside of the bedspread, cut out a large rectangular patch from the remaining Fabric 3 to place in the middle of the white cotton backing fabric. Turn under the raw edges of the patch to neaten, then press. Lay the white backing

fabric on your work surface, right side uppermost; place the patch in the centre of the backing fabric, using a tape measure to ensure it is centred. Pin then machine topstitch in place.

8. Lay the completed patchwork panel on your work surface, face down. Centre the backing fabric on top, its right side uppermost, so the wrong sides of the two pieces are facing. Bring the excess Fabric 1 on the sides of the patchwork piece round to enclose the side edges of the backing fabric. Pin to the backing fabric, turning under the long raw edges. Hand stitch or machine topstitch.

9. To finish the bedspread, take the two remaining long strips of Fabric 3. Lay one strip face down on the patchwork side of the bedspread, 7.5cm (3in) down

from the top edge, its ends extending slightly beyond the bedspread. Pin then machine stitch along the 12mm (½in) seam allowance.

10. Open out the strip towards the top edge of the bedspread and press. Turn under the short ends of the strip before folding the strip over the top edge to the underside of the bedspread to enclose all the raw edges. Pin the edges of the strip all round to the backing fabric and hand stitch. Finish the bottom edge of the bedspread in the same way.

Silk-upholstered chair

The appeal of this reproduction French chair is its pretty shape and good lines. Painted in a soft grey/green to coordinate with the new sumptuous silk upholstery, the frame has been painted then sanded to give it an aged appearance and to accentuate the carved decoration.

A MORNING

You will need

100 grade sandpaper

Chair in need of renovation

2.5cm (1in) household paintbrush

White acrylic primer undercoat

Small quantity (tester pot) of flat, non-acrylic emulsion paint in soft grey/green

Antiquing materials (optional – see text below)

2m (2¼yd) checked silk, 122cm (48in) wide

Sharp scissors

Tape measure

Long glass-headed pins

Staple gun and staples

Long length of upholstery braid

Hot glue gun and glue stick

If you prefer more of an antique look than that shown here, there are two options for giving your chair an antique finish after it has been painted. Either use a soft cloth to rub the chair with a dark wax furniture polish (see Step 7, Glazed Cupboard, page 20) or, better still, make up an antiquing liquid as follows. Squeeze 2.5cm (1in) of raw umber artist's oil tube paint into a small jam jar. Add 1–2 tablespoons of white spirit and mix well. Paint this antiquing liquid over the paintwork, leave for 5 minutes, then remove from the top surfaces first using plenty of kitchen paper, allowing the liquid to remain in the little crevices and indentations to look like dust and dirt that has gathered over the years. Keep removing the liquid until the kitchen paper appears clean. The antiquing liquid will have knocked back the colour, making the paintwork appear softer and older. Leave to dry overnight. The next day apply two coats of a good-quality semi-matt oil-based furniture varnish or polyurethane lacquer, allowing sufficient drying time between coats.

1. Using 100 grade sandpaper and always working in the same direction as the grain of wood, rub down the chair frame to reveal the carving, the edges and the lovely lines of the chair. Remove all the wood dust and wipe clean.

2. Using a 2.5cm (1in) household paintbrush, paint the frame with slightly thinned acrylic primer undercoat. Leave to dry before applying a second coat.

3. Rub the top surfaces of the carving and the edges again with sandpaper and wipe away the paint dust.

4. Apply two coats of the emulsion top coat, allowing the first coat to dry before applying the second. When the paint is dry, again rub the paint through on the top surfaces with sandpaper to give the appearance of age. Remove all the dust and wipe clean. (You could now antique the frame, as described above, if you prefer an aged look.)

RE-COVERING THE SEAT

5. Lay the fabric, its pattern running diagonally, across the seat. Cut a piece of silk following the shape of the seat and approximately 5cm (2in) larger all round. Push pins into the seat to hold the fabric in position then staple its edges to the frame, pulling the fabric taut as you work around the seat.

6. Cover both sides of the chair back in the same way. (The inside chair back of the chair pictured had a shaped and padded piece, which fitted on first. The silk was stapled over it on to the frame.)

7. Cut two small oval pieces of silk, again on the bias, for the small arm pads. You may find it easier to turn under the raw edges of these small, awkwardly shaped pieces before stapling them to the wooden arm rests, in the same way as before.

8. Finally, measure and cut to length the braid required to trim the seat, the arm pads and both sides of the chair back, allowing extra to turn under the ends each time. Hot glue the braid trim in place over the staples and the raw edges of the silk upholstery; the glue prevents the raw edges from fraying.

Silk-covered headboard

A comfortable king-size bed with an outdated pine headboard was crying out for this complete makeover. The bedroom's neutral tones provided the perfect backdrop for the soft grey/green painted headboard – the colour inspired by the lichen green stripe in the silk used to re-cover the headboard and for the King-Size Silk Bedspread (see page 96).

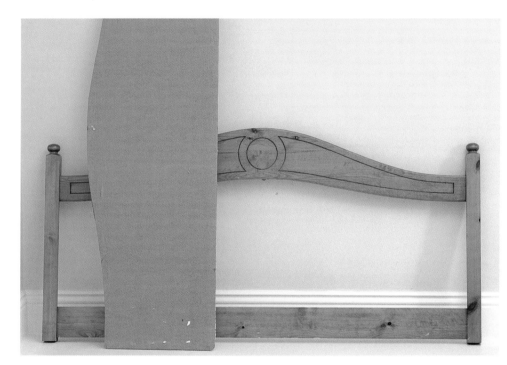

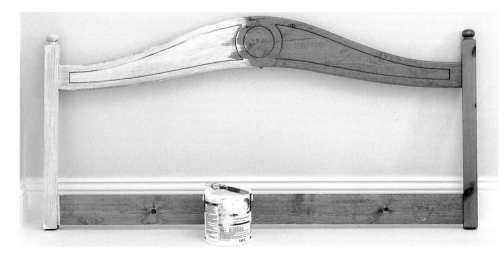

You will need

Bed with wooden headboard
100 grade sandpaper
2.5cm (1in) paintbrush
White acrylic primer undercoat
Small quantity (tester pot) of
        flat, non-acrylic emulsion
        paint in soft grey/green
Tape measure
Sharp scissors
Approx. 2m (2¼yd) checked silk,
        122cm (48in) wide,
        allowing for a pattern
        match of 22cm (8½in)
Long glass-headed pins
Sewing machine
Staple gun and staples
0.5m (½yd) damson silk
Needle and matching thread
Clear fabric glue or hot glue
        gun and glue stick
Length of lining fabric

1. Remove the headboard from
the bed then remove the padded
insert section. Using 100 grade
sandpaper and working in the
same direction as the wood grain,
sand the headboard to form a
good key on which to paint.
Remove the dust and wipe clean.

2. With the headboard against a
wall or flat on a protected work
surface, apply a coat of slightly
thinned acrylic primer undercoat.
Leave to dry before applying a
second and possibly a third coat.
Turn the headboard over to paint
the other side. Leave to dry.

3. Next, apply two coats of the
emulsion top coat all over,
allowing the first coat to dry
before applying the second.

COVERING THE PADDED HEADBOARD INSERT

4. Measure the padded headboard insert – you need a rectangle of silk large enough to cover it and to fold over to the underside where it can be stapled. Since your fabric is unlikely to be the full width of the headboard, you will probably need to join widths. To avoid a seam down the centre of the headboard, plan to have a whole width of fabric in the middle of the headboard and attach half or whole widths on either side of this piece. Allow extra fabric for a 1.5cm (⅝in) seam allowance on each edge to be joined, and for matching large patterns.
Pin the side sections to the central width of fabric, right sides facing. Pin then machine stitch. Open out the joined fabric and press the seams open.

5. Place the padded insert on a work surface, its right side facing

up. Lay the fabric over it. Secure in place with pins pushed into the padding on the outer edges, ensuring the fabric's pattern stays centred and straight.

6. Turn the padded insert over and staple the excess fabric to the back of the insert in a few key places to hold it firm. Continue stapling the fabric in place, pulling it fairly taut as you work (the silk pictured has a slightly 'seersucker ' or rumpled stripe, which makes this more difficult to achieve). When the fabric is stapled all round make sure the padded insert will fit back into its frame. Trim the silk's raw edges.

7. To make the trimming, cut two long strips of damson silk, 10cm (4in) wide and long enough to wrap comfortably over the padded insert. (Stitch shorter strips together if necessary, end to end, to achieve the desired length, pressing any joining

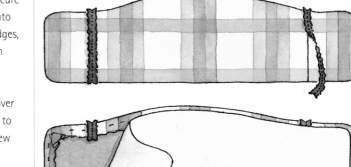

seams open). Turn under the ends of each strip to neaten, then press the long raw edges under and then towards each other to meet in the centre, overlapping one long edge slightly with the other – this will be the back of the trimming. Pin in place then neatly hand or machine stitch.

8. Using damson-coloured thread doubled for strength, secure the thread well at one end of each strip by oversewing a few stitches then sew neatly along the centre of the strips using a loose running stitch. Draw the fabric along the thread to gather it and make the ruched trimming. Secure the thread firmly when the gathering is finished.

9. Pin the ruched trimming strips to the fabric-covered padded insert, directly over the machine-stitched seams. Staple the top end of each trimming at the back of the padded insert. Using a clear fabric glue or hot glue gun, stick the trimming to the seam lines. Finish by stapling the bottom end of each trimming to the back of the padded insert, as before.

10. If you would like the back of the headboard to look neat and stay less dusty, cut a piece of lining fabric to shape, allowing an extra 2cm (¾in) all round to turn under. Staple or hot glue the lining in place, over the staples and the raw edges of the silk.

11. Replace the covered headboard on the bed, screwing it firmly into position.

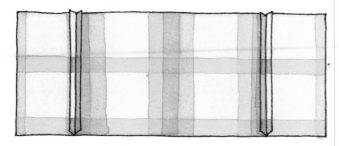

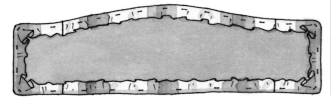

King-sized silk bedspread

This beautiful decorative bedspread matches the Silk-Covered Headboard (see page 92). The newly covered headboard needs to be in place for this project so that the patterned silk used for the headboard and the bedspread can be matched up exactly. Otherwise, when the bedspread is on the bed you will find it irritating if the patterned stripes do not all line up.

A DAY

You will need

Tape measure
Sharp scissors
5.5m (6yd) checked silk, 122cm
    (48in) wide, allowing for a
    pattern match of 22cm (8½in)
Long glass-headed pins
Sewing machine

Silk always seems very special, the texture so pleasurable as it reflects the light and when the fabric is 'scrunched up' it has even better reflective qualities. I always enjoyed wearing silk-lined suits and full silk skirts for the luxurious swishing sounds they made with the slightest movement.

I hope you will find the lovely soft colours of the fabric used here and the very simple design of this project appealing. The other stronger colourways are fabulous, too, and the wonderful thing is that they all mix and match beautifully.

1. Cut a full width of silk 2.5m (98in) long. If you are making the bedspread to complement the

Silk-Covered Headboard (see page 92), lay the silk on the bed in order to match the striped pattern with that on the newly covered headboard.

2. Cut a second 2.5m (98in) length for the side sections of the bedspread, remembering that this piece will be cut in half lengthways and the checked pattern has to match along both long side edges of the central bedspread section.

3. Lay the side and centre sections with their right sides facing once you have matched up the stripes exactly. Pin in place then machine stitch. If you have any doubts as to how well you have matched the pattern then baste the sections in place first.

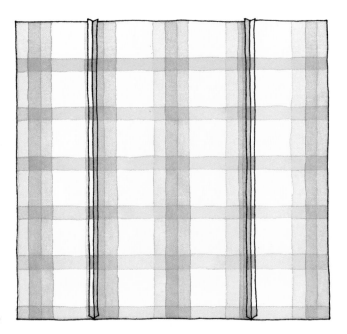

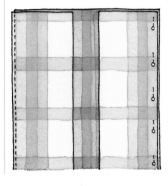

4. Open out the stitched panel of fabric. Press open the seams and machine zigzag stitch along the raw edges of the side seams to prevent the silk fraying.

5. Turn under a double hem all the way around the bedspread, pin and hand stitch invisibly. Arrange your finished bedspread on the bed and admire!

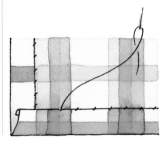

Rose-trimmed curtains

You don't have to be outdoors to enjoy the beauty of roses as you will find some wonderful rose-printed fabrics to bring into your home. The gorgeous full-blown, old-fashioned roses on the exquisite chintz fabric used for these curtain borders bring a breath of summer into the room.

A DAY

You will need

Length of rose-patterned chintz, 137cm (54in) wide
Sharp scissors
Tape measure
Long glass-headed pins
Straight edge (optional)
Light pencil
2 large finely woven, ivory or ecru-coloured antique linen sheets
Sewing machine
Length of lining fabric
Curtain heading tape
Needle and matching thread

For this project the least amount of chintz was used to the greatest effect with the aim of achieving the look of sumptuous full-blown roses in the bedroom. If you have sufficient fabric to make the entire curtains using the chintz alone, and to allow for the pattern to match when the curtains are drawn, then so much the better.

Both the ecru linen and the chintz are of the finest quality and hang beautifully. I just couldn't resist displaying the little *cachepot*, decorated with almost identical roses, on the windowsill.

1. Lay the chintz on a large work surface and cut to the required length, allowing an extra 5cm (2in) to turn over at the top of the curtain plus sufficient to make the hem.

2. Measure to find the middle of the width of fabric. Using pins or a straight edge and a light pencil, mark a cutting line down the full length of the chintz. Following the cutting line, cut the chintz in half lengthways to make the two border strips. Lightly pencil distinguishing marks on the back of each strip of chintz so that you remember which is for the left-hand curtain and which for the right, so the pattern on the two borders will match up when the curtains are drawn. It is all too easy to end up using the wrong strip, the wrong way up!

3. To make the right-hand curtain first, lay a linen sheet on your work surface, right side uppermost. Lay the right-hand half of the rose chintz face down on the sheet, aligning its selvage against the edge of the sheet. Pin then machine stitch the two pieces of fabric together. Press open the seam.

4. Turn under 5cm (2in) all across the top edge of the curtain and then pin to hold the fabric in place temporarily.

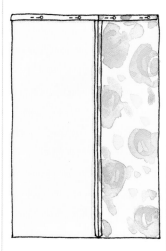

5. Measure and cut out the lining fabric for both curtains, allowing an extra 5cm (2in) to turn over at the top plus sufficient to turn up the hem. You may require 1½–2 widths to line each curtain, depending upon the width of the sheets being used. Pin then machine stitch together the pieces required for each curtain. Press open the seams. Press under 5cm (2in) across the top edge.

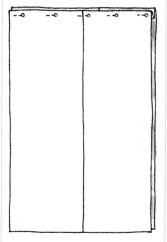

6. Lay the curtain face down on the work surface. Lay the lining fabric, right side uppermost, on top of the curtain, placing its neatened top edge just below the pinned top edge of the main curtain. Gradually remove the pins from the curtain as you work and use them to secure the lining fabric to the curtain along the top edge.

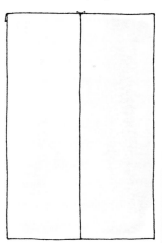

7. Turn under the lining at the sides of the curtain. Turn under the long side edge of the chintz to neaten it then fold 4–5cm (1½–2in) to the back of the curtain, around the edge of the lining fabric. Neaten the other long side edge of the curtain similarly. Pin both side edges of the lining and chintz together, then hand stitch and press.

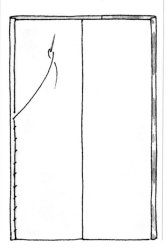

8. Cut the heading tape slightly longer than the width of the curtain. Turning under each raw end of the tape, position the tape across the top edge of the curtain, again removing the pins and replacing them to hold all the layers together. Machine stitch all around the edge of the heading tape to attach it to the curtain, remembering to stitch over the draw-cords at the chintz end of the tape to secure them. Keep the cords at the other end of the tape out of the way as you stitch so that they remain loose.

9. Measure the desired curtain length accurately before marking with pins and turning up the hem to enclose the bottom edge of the lining. It may help to press the turning first; if not, press the curtain when it is finished. Hemstitch by hand then gather the curtain along the draw-cords to the required width. Knot the draw-cords securely – do not cut them or you will never be able to flatten the curtain for cleaning.

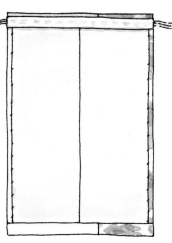

10. Complete the left-hand curtain in the same way, ensuring you use the chintz the same way up as for the first curtain.

Pot cupboard

A renovated French pot cupboard makes a perfect bedside cupboard or useful occasional table for a lamp.

A WEEKEND

You will need

Old French pot cupboard in need of renovation
Piece of plywood, cut to size
100 grade sandpaper
2.5cm (1in) household paintbrush
White acrylic primer undercoat
Small quantity of matt emulsion paint in green or a flat, non-acrylic emulsion paint in a colour from a heritage range
Dark antique wax polish
Soft cloth
Tape measure
Sharp scissors
Fabric remnant to match paintwork
Hot glue gun and glue stick or staple gun and staples

This little pot cupboard was discovered at a *brocante* fair in a French village. It was in poor condition but had potential! The drawer needed new runners and plywood was cut to fit the top recess which had originally housed marble. Fabric now covers the plywood top – this could be protected by a square of plate glass cut to size if liked.

1. Begin by removing any handles from your cupboard that are not to be painted and check the piece of plywood for the top fits in place. Using 100 grade sandpaper, and always working in the same direction as the grain of wood (whether it is painted or not), sand the cupboard by hand

to form a good key on which to paint. Remove the dust using a vacuum cleaner then wipe clean.

2. Using a 2.5cm (1in) household paintbrush, paint the outside of the cupboard with acrylic primer undercoat. Leave to dry before applying a second coat. (There is no need to paint the inside, apart from the area just inside the door and along the door edges, since old French pot cupboards are lined with porcelain.)

3. When the second coat of undercoat is completely dry, sand back the edges of the cupboard top and doors, the reeded legs and door panel to simulate wear.

4. Apply a slightly thinned coat of green matt emulsion paint; leave to dry. Apply a second coat if necessary. Sand back the edges

of the cupboard as before, again to produce an aged look.

5. When the paint is completely dry, gently rub antique wax polish over the paintwork, using a soft cloth and working with the grain to tone down the 'newness' of the paint. Leave for 10 minutes before buffing to remove the excess wax.

6. Cut a piece of fabric to cover the plywood top with about 7cm (3in) extra all round for turning under. Lay the fabric on a work surface, wrong side uppermost. Place the plywood on top and bring the edges of the fabric up over the plywood. Hot glue or staple the fabric tightly in place, trimming excess fabric from the corners. Replace the cupboard handles and insert the fabric-covered plywood top in place.

Victorian linen cupboard

Just one roll of exquisite Regency rose wallpaper, discovered at an antiques fair, is enough to give a lift to a lovely, cream-painted Victorian pine cupboard. Painting the beading around the door panels creates a frame for each panel of wallpaper, the colour of the paint chosen to coordinate perfectly with the wallpaper.

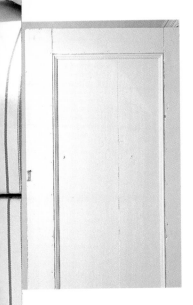 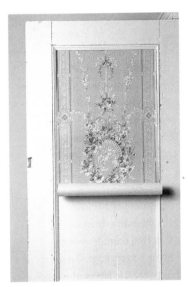 

3. Cut out each panel of paper, one at a time. Use small pieces of reusable adhesive in the top corners of each panel to check the fit of the wallpaper. Take care if your paper is old as it will tear and smudge easily.

4. Working with one piece of paper at a time, apply wallpaper paste evenly over it, brushing paste out over the edges to ensure complete coverage. Attach the paper to the panel. Using a soft cloth, gently pat the surface of the paper and smooth it down, taking care in case the surface colours smudge. Leave all the panels to dry completely.

5. Fill a jam jar with water. Squeeze a little of each of the artist's acrylic tube paints on to the lid. Dip an artist's brush or fitch in the water and use it to mix up the required colour of paint for the door panel mouldings. Paint the mouldings and leave to dry.

2 DAYS

You will need

Tape measure
Old cupboard in need of
    renovation
Roll of wallpaper
Pencil
Ruler or straight edge
Sharp scissors
Reusable adhesive
Small tub of ready mixed wallpaper
    paste

Small brush
Soft cloth
Jam jar with lid
Artist's acrylic tube paints in
    ultramarine, titanium
    white and Payne's grey
No. 8 artist's paintbrush or
    fitch

1. First, measure the size of each individual door panel accurately since they inevitably vary in shape and size on an old cupboard.

2. Partially unroll the wallpaper on a clean work surface or the floor. Stand a couple of heavy items at the corners of the paper to anchor it and another further down to prevent it rolling up. Transpose the measurements accurately on to the paper, centring the wallpaper design as best you can. Draw a faint pencil line as a cutting guide, as long as it will not be visible later, or pencil a series of faint dots, using a ruler or straight edge as a guide.

the interlining all around the sides to give the ottoman a padded appearance.

3. To determine the length of red-and-cream striped ticking required to cover the outside of the ottoman, measure from the underside of the base, up the side, over the top edge and at least 2.5cm (1in) down from the top on the inside. Cut a full width of fabric to this measurement. (A fabric width, with its selvages turned under, may be enough to cover the front and part of both ends of the ottoman; this would mean only two 'seams' – one each end of the box.)

Ensure the stripes are perfectly vertical before stapling the fabric in place close to the

inside top edge and on the underside of the ottoman. Turn the selvages under and staple these neatened edges down the sides of the ottoman.

4. Pleat the fabric neatly at the corners, top and bottom, pulling it tightly in order to staple it down.

5. Now that you have seen how far one piece of ticking will go, cut another two or three pieces to length as necessary, depending on the size of your ottoman. Begin by matching up the stripes exactly and overlapping the fabric where you left off – turn under the selvage plus another 5cm (2in) but staple this overlapping edge of fabric at

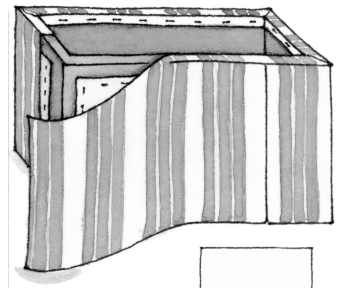

the top and bottom edges of the ottoman only, out of sight. If you pull the fabric tight enough, it should remain in position; if it does not, you can hand stitch the overlapping edge 'invisibly' (remember to wear a thimble).

6. If you need to use more than two widths of fabric, add the last section of fabric by starting in the same way as the second, but it may be easier to cut the piece (with a seam allowance) so that it finishes at a corner where it can be hand stitched neatly and unobtrusively to the fabric beneath it.

7. For the lining, measure the dimensions of the interior of the ottoman. Cut four pieces – two for the inside ends of the box and two for the front and back inside – adding seam allowances on the side and bottom edges of each piece and 2.5cm (1in) for a turning along the top edge. Pin then machine stitch the four pieces together in the correct sequence to make one long strip. Trim the seams.

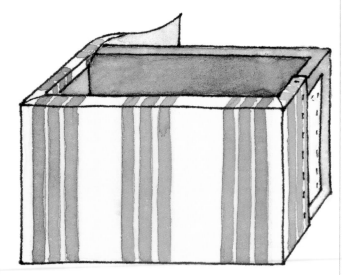

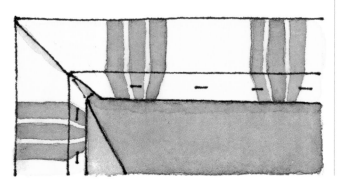

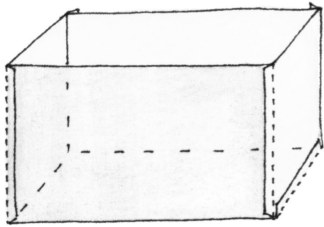

8. Cut a rectangle of lining fabric for the bottom of the ottoman inside, again adding seam allowances all round. Pin then machine stitch this piece to the bottom edge of the long strip. Stitch the remaining side seam to end up with an open 'box' of fabric. Trim the seams.

9. Place the shaped lining inside the ottoman, its raw seams against the sides of the ottoman. Anchor the fabric at the bottom of the ottoman with a staple at each corner. Make sure the fabric is taut as you pin the turned-under top edge of the lining fabric over the striped ticking, about 12mm–2.5cm (½–1in) down from the top of the box. Stitch neatly by hand (the best option) or alternatively you could hot glue it in place.

10. Now turn your attention to the lid of the ottoman. Restaple intact but sagging webbing if possible; replace damaged webbing with new. If the lid is flat and uncomfortable, place a large feather pillow on top of the lid and staple the edges of its cover to the frame to hold it firmly in position.

11. Measure from underneath the lid and over the top to the other side, to determine the

amount of red-and-cream striped ticking required to cover it. Allow extra fabric for matching the pattern with the fabric covering the body of the ottoman.

12. Lay the fabric, wrong side uppermost, on the work surface. Place the upside-down lid on top of the fabric. Pin the fabric in place temporarily, adjusting where necessary until the stripes on the lid align with those on the sides of the box. When you are satisfied with the positioning, staple the ticking carefully on to the frame on the underside of the

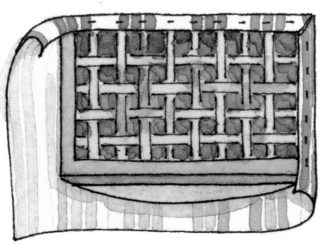

lid, checking regularly that the stripes are still aligned. Make a neat pleat at each corner as you did when covering the body of the ottoman.

13. If you were unable to remove the old hinges from the lid, make four angled incisions at the corners of each hinge. Turn under the fabric and sew or stick it neatly around each hinge.

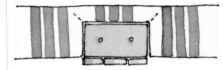

14. Cut a piece of lining fabric to fit the inside of the lid, adding 2.5cm (1in) all round for turning the edges under. Press under the edges; pin then neatly hand stitch the fabric in position, over the edge of the ticking.

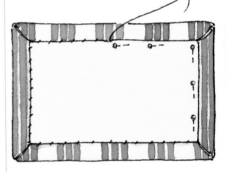

15. Lastly, reattach the hinges if you removed them, driving the screws through the fabric into the original holes – if they have moved position for any reason, bore new holes using a bradawl before inserting the screws.

Director's chair with heart cushion

Old director's chairs can easily be repainted and decked out in new hard-wearing canvas or heavy cotton fabric for use in a conservatory or for alfresco dining. For extra colour and comfort add cushions made from machine-dyed old linen sheets and trimmed with inexpensive heavy cotton checks.

DIRECTOR'S CHAIR – 2 HOURS

You will need

Director's chair to be re-covered
Old screwdriver and pincers
Sharp scissors
1m (1yd) cotton drill, duck or canvas or other heavy-duty fabric
Tape measure
Matt emulsion paint in a colour of your choice
2.5cm (1in) household paintbrush
Hammer and upholstery pins or carpet tacks, or a staple gun and staples

1. Director's chairs vary slightly in design. If the design of yours makes it necessary to remove the chair back in order to access the fabric, undo the wing nuts on the chair back to remove it. Unroll the old fabric back to the nails or staples; lever them up and pull them out, using an old screwdriver and pincers.

2. Accessing the fabric of the chair seat may be a bit more fiddly. The trick is to lift the chair up on to a work surface and fold (or unfold) it into the best position – perhaps upside down – whatever proves to be the easiest. Remove the nails or staples as before – you might have to cut away the old fabric first.

3. Cut two pieces from the new fabric to exactly the same shape and size as the old chair back and seat pieces.

4. Paint the chair with at least two coats of matt emulsion paint, allowing it to dry thoroughly between coats. Fold and unfold the chair in every direction to check that all the surfaces have been repainted.

5. When all the woodwork is completely dry, attach the new fabric using a hammer and upholstery pins or tacks or using a staple gun. Ensure the seat is firmly fixed – you do not want any embarrassing mishaps!

HEART CUSHION – 1 HOUR

You will need

Paper
Pencil
Tape measure
Sharp scissors
Long glass-headed pins
Two 12.5cm (5in) squares of red-and-white checked fabric
Needle and matching thread
Loose dried lavender
Short length of ricrac or ribbon
Ready-made piped or pleated-edge square cushion (see text below)
Red button

To enhance your director's chair, first make basic cushions following the directions for Piped Ticking Cushion and Pleated-Edge Cushion (see pages 50–53). For the main fabric for the cushion covers use heavyweight coarsely woven linen, perhaps part of a worn or discoloured sheet, and dye it using a navy blue hot-

water washing-machine dye, following the manufacturer's directions. For the cushions' pleated or piped edges, use a red-and-white checked heavy Indian cotton. The cushions can then be decorated with this lavender-filled heart.

1. Fold a sheet of paper in half and draw half a heart shape, approximately 12.5 x 12.5cm (5 x 5in), against the folded edge. Cut out the template and open out the paper heart.

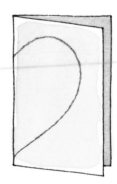

2. Pin the paper heart on to the red-and-white checked fabric. Cut out two fabric heart shapes. Discard the paper template.

3. Pin and sew the heart shapes together, right sides facing, leaving a small opening through which to insert the dried lavender.

4. Turn the fabric the right side out. Fill the heart with dried lavender then turn in the seam allowances and stitch the opening closed. Stitch a loop of ricrac or ribbon to the top of the lavender-filled heart, sew a red button onto the finished square cushion and hang the loop of the heart over the button to attach.

Brightened-up basket chair

Repaint an old Lloyd Loom or basket chair then fill it with these comfortable cushions. A white-painted chair is the easiest backdrop for peony red-and-white checks, and this one would look great on the veranda, in the conservatory or kitchen. Just sit back and relax in comfort – especially on sunny days when it is too hot to do anything else!

2 HOURS

You will need

Pencil
Paper
Newly painted basket chair
Sharp scissors
Square of fire-proofed foam,
10cm (4in) thick
Sharp knife with long blade
Length of red-and-white
checked ticking
Tape measure
Long glass-headed pins
Sewing machine
Needle and matching thread
2 square cushion pads

Fireproof foam can be purchased from upholstery suppliers, large fabric shops and market traders. Good quality heavy cotton fabrics in a wide range of colours are sold by market traders, or look in department stores. Look out for old wicker or Lloyd Loom chairs at auction and car boot sales – transform them by brushing or spraying on a few coats of paint.

1. Using pencil and paper, make a template of the shape of the chair seat. Cut out the template and use it to cut the foam to the correct shape.

2. Spread out the red-and-white checked ticking on a work surface. Lay the foam on top and make sure the checks are square with the front edge of the foam. Mark out the shape of the foam, adding a seam allowance of 2cm (³⁄₄in) all round. Cut out two pieces of ticking – for the top and bottom of the cushion.

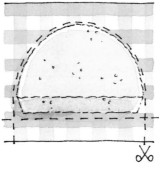

3. Measure around the outside of the cushion to determine the length of fabric required for the cushion gusset. Add an extra 2.5cm (1in) to allow for the side seam. Cut a strip of fabric to this

length and 14cm (5¹⁄₂in) wide, which allows for a seam allowance of 2cm (³⁄₄in) along the top and bottom edges of the gusset. (If necessary, cut two strips for the gusset and stitch them together to make one strip of the required length.)

4. Turn under 12mm (¹⁄₂in) each end of the long gusset strip and press. With right sides facing, pin one long edge of the gusset piece right around the edge of the piece that will be the top of the cushion, leaving the gusset side seam open. Machine stitch.

5. Similarly, pin then machine stitch the other long edge of the gusset piece to the bottom cushion cover piece, but leaving the front edge unstitched for now as well. This allows you to turn the fabric the right side out and insert the unwieldy piece of foam through the opening.

6. Once the foam is inside the cushion cover, turn in the seam

allowances and hand sew the open edges closed with unobtrusive neat stitches.

7. To make the cushions for the chair back, for each cushion cut two squares of fabric 2.5cm (1in) larger all round than the cushion pad. Pin and machine stitch the two squares of fabric together, right sides facing, around three sides of the square. Turn the fabric to the right side. Insert the cushion pad, turn in the raw edges and hand stitch the opening closed.

Directory of suppliers

Antique Bed Centre
27 Mill Street
Oakham, Rutland
Leicestershire
Tel: 01572 724364
Fax: 01572 755094
French and English antique
beds, wood, brass, iron,
upholstered half-testers,
bateau lit, matching pairs, all
with new handmade spring
bases. Full UK delivery
service.

Baer & Ingram Wallpapers & Fabrics
273 Wandsworth Bridge
Road
London SW6 2TX
Tel: 020 7736 6111
Fax: 020 7736 8581
Baer & Ingram by phone:
01373 813800

Beds Are Uzzz
11 Cobham Road
Ferndown Industrial Estate
Wimborne
Dorset BH21 7PE
Tel: 01202 891897
Fax: 01202 870375
Quality beds at discount
prices.

Bedsteads of Bath & Bristol
2 Walcot Buildings
London Road
Bath BA1 6AD
Tel: 01225 339182
Antique and reproduction
brass, iron and wooden beds.

The Bed Workshop
The Old Pickle Factory
Braunton Road
Bedminster, Bristol
Tel: 0117 963 6659
6000 sq ft of restored
French beds, marriage
armoires, cherry and walnut
chests, tables, as well as new
oak, pine and cherry beds at
reasonable prices.

Bennison Fabrics Ltd
16 Holbein Place
London SW1W 8NL
Tel: 020 7730 8076
Fax: 020 7823 4997

Cartouche
32 Salisbury Street
Shaftesbury
Dorset
Tel: 01747 858700
French decorative antiques
at reasonable prices and the
most inspiring textiles and
curtains.

Dmg Antiques Fairs Ltd
P O Box 100
Newark
Nottinghamshire
NG24 1DJ
Tel: 01636 702326
Fax: 01636 707923
Information and dates of
fairs held all over the
country; Newark is the
largest of all the
International Antiques Fairs.

Farrow & Ball
Uddens Trading Estate
Wimborne
Dorset BH21 7NL
Tel: 01202 876141
Fax: 01202 873793
E-mail: farrow-
ball@farrow-ball.co.uk
Website: www.farrow-
ball.co.uk
Manufacturers of traditional
papers and paint. Telephone
order line and credit card
facility – all papers and
paints delivered free of
charge on mainland UK. Fast
delivery service. Large range
of off-whites as well as
National Trust and Archive
ranges.

Georgia Carr
Dartington
Devon
Tel: 01803 866078
Antique textiles; by
appointment only.

Harlequin Fabrics & Wallcoverings Ltd
Ladybird House
Beeches Road
Loughborough
Leicestershire LE11 2HA
Tel: 01509 225000
Fax: 01509 225001
Lovely range of fabrics
including the most
delightful toile de Jouy
Romance fabric 'Summer
Fayre'.

Holman Specialist Paints Ltd
1 Central Trading Estate
Signal Way, Swindon
Wiltshire SN3 1PD
Tel: 01793 511537
Fax: 01793 431142
Wonderful Finnish-made
floor varnishes and
woodstains. 'Supreme' floor
finish is a sealant, colorant
and hard varnish, which
requires no maintenance
other than washing and
keeping clean.

Ian Mankin
271 Wandsworth Bridge
Road
London SW6 2TX
Tel: 020 7371 8825

Ian Mankin
109 Regents Park Road
Primrose Hill
London NW1 8UR
Tel: 020 7722 0997 for
fabric by post.
Huge range of ticking,
cotton, linen and canvas,
checks and stripes,
ginghams.

Jean Monro Ltd
318 Chelsea Harbour Design
Centre
London SW10 0XE
Tel: 020 7376 7215
Fax: 020 7376 7203
E-mail:
sales@jeanmonro.co.uk
The most exquisite range of
floral chintzes, especially
roses and ribbons.

Mill Side Forge
Clear Springs Farm
Stoke Trister
Wincanton
Somerset BA9 9PQ
Tel: 01963 33223
Fax: 01963 33220
Handmade iron beds,
beautifully made iron
curtain poles with a range of
decorative ends made to
measure to fit all types of
windows including bays.
Interesting range of
furniture.

Monkwell Ltd
(incorporating Design
Archives)
10–12 Wharfdale Road
Bournemouth
Dorset BH4 9BT
Tel: 01202 753222 for
information, swatches,
brochures.

Monkwell Ltd
The Decorative Fabrics
Gallery Ltd
322 Kings Road
London SW3
Tel: 020 7823 3294

The Natural Fabric Co.
Wessex Place
127 High Street
Hungerford
Berkshire RG17 0DL
Tel: 01488 684002
Fax: 01488 686455
Large range of cottons,
linens, tickings, ginghams,
chambrays and trims –
swatches available.

The Odd Mattress Factory
Tel: 01772 786666 for details
and price guide. Nationwide
delivery service.
Handmade mattresses –
long or short, broad or thin;
anything can be supplied.

Pavilion Textiles
Elizabeth Baer
Freshford Hall
Freshford
Bath BA3 6EJ
Tel: 01225 722522
Website:
www.allaboutantiques.co.uk/
pavilion/
Specialities French creamy
coarse-woven linen and
hemp sheets and striped
tickings once used on
feather beds. Heirloom
linens, regional and
domestic fabrics and
peasant wear. Table linen
and antique textiles.
Appointment only. UK and
US cash and cheques
accepted. Postage/shipping
extra. No VAT.

**Prestige Upholstery &
Interiors**
Chapel Lodge
East Gomeldon Road
Salisbury
Wiltshire SP4 6NB
Tel: 01980 611223
Quality re-upholstery
service, curtains, cushions
and loose covers, vast range
of fabrics, free no-obligation
estimates. Friendly and
helpful service and excellent
workmanship.

**Real French Farmhouse
Furniture**
Limousin Furniture Company
1a Siegliere
23200 Aubusson
France
Tel: 00 33 555 838 876
Fax: 00 33 555 663 815

Whaleys (Bradford) Ltd
Harris Court
Great Horton, Bradford
West Yorkshire BD7 4EQ
Tel: 01274 576718
Fax: 01274 521309
Website: www.whaleys-
bradford.ltd.uk
Natural linen scrim, white
linen scrim, natural hessians,
curtain lining fabric, heading
tape and probably the
largest range of natural
fabrics at exceptionally
reasonable prices. Swatches
available and fast postal or
carrier service.

Index

Index

Dedication

This book is dedicated to my mother whose excellent eye for antiques, which encompassed fine furniture, paintings and porcelain, kindled my own keen interest at an early age. I was in awe of the huge embroidered tablecloths and the white and drawn threadwork on fine linen sheets she had sewn as a girl! She was – and still is – an expert knitter in the finest wools. Her exquisite tapestries, many chair seats – all 'paintings' in themselves – stools and bell-pulls will one day be much-cherished family heirlooms. Having had to cope alone throughout the War years, she became adept at tackling almost anything – it could and would be done! She also encouraged me to be creative, to paint and sketch, make a puppet theatre, sew and knit. Years later, I was frightfully fashion conscious in my late teens and complicated *Vogue* patterns and materials were purchased for me to make my own suits, dresses and skirts; thank goodness my father was always persuaded to buy my evening dresses! Although we have very different tastes, I know that it was my mother's unique sense of style and colour that taught me a great deal and opened my eyes to the potential of the finished piece! This book is for you, Mother, with my love.

Acknowledgements

My special love and thanks go to Penny Clark and Polly Mobsby for accompanying me to France on a buying trip for this book. Polly's knowledge of textiles and furniture and her strict price guidance was a welcome second opinion, which stopped me getting too carried away. Penny's fluent French eased the way to many a good deal being struck, and she was brilliant at navigating and sharing the driving. It was such good fun and all I can say is 'Encore'!

To Di Lewis who has surpassed herself once more with truly wonderful photography throughout the book. It is always an inspiration to watch such a gifted artist at work – 'seeing' each project as if through the lens – creating such magical photographs.

I am indebted to the following people: Sharon Ashman, my Editor at Hamlyn Octopus, who has been an absolute delight to work with, being constantly pleasant, approachable, unflappable and extremely understanding at all times; Claire Harvey, the designer – good luck in South America; Jo Lethaby, with whom I have worked on the two previous books, and who still retains her patience and sense of fun while making clear sense out of my confusing text in her own meticulous way; Louise Griffiths, the designer, who has also worked on the previous books – thank you very much.

My grateful thanks to the following companies who generously donated their fabrics for projects: Monkwell Ltd for the fabulous checked silks in three colourways and the 'Painted Room Red' voile from the Design Archives range; Nicoletta Nicolaou and her manager Angela Fawcett at The Decorative Fabrics Gallery, now in Kings Road, for their endless help, efficiency and speedy response in getting fabrics for projects to me – much appreciated!; Harlequin Fabrics & Wallcoverings Ltd (Alison Gore) for the delightful blue and white toile de Jouy Romance fabric 'Summer Fayre'; Jean Monro Ltd for the exquisite 'Autumn Roses' chintz; Bennison Fabrics Ltd for the two lovely 'faded' rose designs from their 'East Coast' collection.

My thanks also to the following companies whose products enhanced the book: Ian Mankin – tickings and gingham; Beds Are Uzzz at Ferndown for a mattress to fit the French day bed; Whaleys (Bradford) Ltd for many swatches, advice and all the natural fabrics; Colin Holman of Holman Specialist Paints Ltd for his helpful advice on how to paint a floor etc. Lastly, thanks to Prestige Upholstery & Interiors for their excellent work, and in particular Andrew Pont for collecting and delivering miles out of his way and getting everything organized speedily and efficiently.